Conquest of the Balkans

By the Editors of Time-Life Books

Alexandria, Virginia

TIME
LIFE ®

Time-Life Books Inc.
is a wholly owned subsidiary of

The Time Inc. Book Company

President and Chief Executive Officer:
Kelso F. Sutton
President, Time Inc. Books Direct:
Christopher T. Linen

Time-Life Books Inc.

EDITOR: George Constable
Executive Editor: Ellen Phillips
Director of Design: Louis Klein
Director of Editorial Resources: Phyllis K. Wise
Editorial Board: Russell B. Adams, Jr., Dale M.
Brown, Roberta Conlan, Thomas H. Flaherty,
Lee Hassig, Jim Hicks, Donia Ann Steele,
Rosalind Stubenberg
Director of Photography and Research:
John Conrad Weiser

PRESIDENT: John M. Fahey, Jr.
Senior Vice Presidents: Robert M. DeSena, James
L. Mercer, Paul R. Stewart, Curtis G. Viebranz,
Joseph J. Ward
Vice Presidents: Stephen L. Bair, Bonita L.
Boezeman, Stephen L. Goldstein, Juanita T.
James, Andrew P. Kaplan, Trevor Lunn, Susan J.
Maruyama, Robert H. Smith
Supervisor of Quality Control: James King

PUBLISHER: Joseph J. Ward

The Cover: German troops celebrate the capture
of Athens by raising their battle flag over the
Acropolis on April 27, 1941. Having overrun
Yugoslavia and Greece in just three weeks, the
Wehrmacht next set its sights on Crete, where a
British and Commonwealth command braced
for the storm.

This volume is one of a series that chronicles
the rise and eventual fall of Nazi Germany. Other
books in the series include:
The SS
Fists of Steel
Storming to Power
The New Order
The Reach for Empire
Lightning War
Wolf Packs

The Third Reich

SERIES DIRECTOR: Thomas H. Flaherty
Series Administrator: Jane Edwin
Editorial Staff for *Conquest of the Balkans:*
Designer: Raymond Ripper
Picture Editor: Jane Jordan
Text Editors: Stephen G. Hyslop, John Newton,
Henry Woodhead
Researchers: Kirk E. Denkler (principal), Robin
Currie, Trudy Pearson
Assistant Designer: Lorraine D. Rivard
Copy Coordinator: Charles J. Hagner
Picture Coordinator: Ruth Moss
Editorial Assistant: Jayne A. L. Dover

Special Contributors: George Daniels, Lydia
Preston Hicks, Thomas A. Lewis, Richard W.
Murphy, Brian C. Pohanka (text); Martha-Lee
Beckington, Lisa Champelli, Ann-Louise Gates,
Oobie Gleysteen (research); Michael Kalen Smith
(index)

Editorial Operations
Copy Chief: Diane Ullius
Production: Celia Beattie
Library: Louise D. Forstall

Computer Composition: Gordon E. Buck
(Manager), Deborah G. Tait, Monika D. Thayer,
Janet Barnes Syring, Lillian Daniels

Correspondents: Elisabeth Kraemer-Singh
(Bonn), Christina Lieberman (New York), Maria
Vincenza Aloisi (Paris), Ann Natanson (Rome).
Valuable assistance was also provided by:
Elizabeth Brown (New York), Lesley Coleman
(London), Barbara Hicks (London), Pavle Svabic
(Belgrade), Ann Wise (Rome).

First printing. Printed in U.S.A.

Published simultaneously in Canada.
School and library distribution by Silver Burdett
Company, Morristown, New Jersey 07960.

TIME-LIFE is a trademark of Time Warner Inc.
U.S.A.

**Library of Congress Cataloging in
Publication Data**
Conquest of the Balkans / by the editors of
Time-Life Books.
     p.   cm. — (The Third Reich.)
Bibliography: p.
Includes index.
ISBN 0-8094-6979-0
ISBN 0-8094-6980-4 (lib. bdg.)
   1. World War, 1939–1945—Campaigns—Balkan
Peninsula. 2. World War, 1939–1945—Cam-
paigns—Yugoslavia. 3. World War, 1939–1945—
Campaigns—Greece. I. Time-Life Books.
II. Series.
D766.C58 1990   940.54'21—dc20   89-5062

Other Publications:

AMERICAN COUNTRY
VOYAGE THROUGH THE UNIVERSE
THE TIME-LIFE GARDENER'S GUIDE
MYSTERIES OF THE UNKNOWN
TIME FRAME
FIX IT YOURSELF
FITNESS, HEALTH & NUTRITION
SUCCESSFUL PARENTING
HEALTHY HOME COOKING
UNDERSTANDING COMPUTERS
LIBRARY OF NATIONS
THE ENCHANTED WORLD
THE KODAK LIBRARY OF CREATIVE PHOTOGRAPHY
GREAT MEALS IN MINUTES
THE CIVIL WAR
PLANET EARTH
COLLECTOR'S LIBRARY OF THE CIVIL WAR
THE EPIC OF FLIGHT
THE GOOD COOK
WORLD WAR II
HOME REPAIR AND IMPROVEMENT
THE OLD WEST

For information on and a full description of any
of the Time-Life Books series listed above, please
call 1-800-621-7026 or write:
Reader Information
Time-Life Customer Service
P.O. Box C-32068
Richmond, Virginia 23261-2068

General Consultants

Col. John R. Elting, USA (Ret.), former asso-
ciate professor at West Point, has written or
edited some twenty books, including *Swords
around a Throne, The Superstrategists,* and
American Army Life, as well as *Battles for
Scandinavia* in the Time-Life Books World
War II series. He was chief consultant to the
Time-Life series, The Civil War.

Charles V. P. von Luttichau is an associate at
the U.S. Army Center of Military History in
Washington, D.C., and coauthor of *Command Decision* and *Great Battles.* From 1937
to 1945, he served in the German air force
and taught at the Air Force Academy in Berlin. After the war, he emigrated to the United
States and was a historian in the Office of the
Chief of Military History, Department of the
Army, from 1951 to 1986, when he retired.

Williamson Murray is a professor of European military history at Ohio State University
and has been a visiting professor at the Naval
War College. He has written numerous arti-
cles and books on military affairs, including
The Luftwaffe, 1933-1944, and *The Change in
the European Balance of Power, 1938-1939.*
He has also coedited the three-volume
study, *Military Effectiveness.*

Contents

ONE

Maneuvering in a Diplomatic Minefield

A dolf Hitler learned that the Italians were invading Greece as his train passed through Bologna en route to Florence. The report prompted a bitter tirade. Among his aides, the mood grew as wintry as the snowy alpine landscape the train had recently traversed. Yet just an hour or two later, Hitler appeared remarkably composed when he was compelled to hear the news again, this time from Benito Mussolini himself. "Führer, we are marching!" cried the duce as he welcomed Hitler to Florence. "This morning, a victorious Italian army has crossed the Greek frontier!"

The date was October 28, 1940. Standing on the gaily decorated station platform that chill morning, Hitler congratulated his ally on his bold venture—an attack the Führer had just denounced to his aides as impetuous and premature. Although he would admit none of his misgivings to Mussolini, Hitler believed the Italian leader was not only risking defeat—for the Greeks were staunch fighters—but threatening the delicate balance of power in the Balkans that Germany had worked so hard to achieve. The British would surely attempt to aid Greece, and other Balkan states might be drawn into the fray. If that happened, Hitler would have to commit German forces, a development he wanted at all costs to avoid. He had no concern for the people of the Balkans—he called Germany's Balkan allies in World War I *Gerümpel*, or trash. But without their tacit support, or at least their guaranteed neutrality, he knew his most ambitious plans of conquest were bound to fail. Whether he liked it or not, he was inextricably involved with a complex and fractious region that the nineteenth-century German statesman Otto von Bismarck had once proclaimed was "not worth the bones of a single Pomeranian grenadier."

In fact, the mountainous, strife-torn Balkan peninsula—embracing Rumania, Bulgaria, Yugoslavia, Albania, Greece, and a small part of Turkey—held a pivotal strategic position as both a bridge and a buffer between east and west. And outside interest in the area was only intensified by the knowledge that beneath its stark surface lay abundant natural resources—petroleum, chrome, manganese, copper, and other raw materials coveted

A poker-faced Adolf Hitler flanks a smiling Benito Mussolini on the balcony of the Palazzo Vecchio in Florence on October 28, 1940. The news that Italy had invaded Greece earlier that day angered Hitler, who was wary of entanglements in the Balkans. But he chose to mask his dismay rather than risk a breach with his ally. As an aide noted, the Führer did his best to conceal his "mental gnashing of teeth."

by the industrial powers for their war machines. Already in the twentieth century, conflict in the Balkans had sparked one world war. Now the region would once more be a crucible in which opposing nations tested their will.

The crisis in the Balkans confronted Hitler at a critical juncture in his drive to dominate Europe. To be sure, his Wehrmacht had shattered six Allied armies in three lightning campaigns, giving him an empire that stretched from Warsaw to Brest and from the Alps to beyond the Arctic Circle. But he still faced a basic strategic problem. Now as before, he was hemmed in by one potentially powerful adversary in the west and another in the east. France had been defeated, but Britain remained defiant, and behind Britain loomed the threat of American power. In the east, the Soviet Union was reassembling an officer corps decimated in the Stalinist purges and pushing ahead with an arms buildup comparable to Germany's own. The specter of a two-front war continued to haunt the German high command.

Hitler had been expected to invade England soon after the capitulation of France in June of 1940. Indeed, he had signed the order for such an invasion, code-named Operation Sea Lion, in mid-July. Yet he harbored serious doubts about the plan, and within a few weeks he issued a second directive making the invasion conditional upon the success of the Luftwaffe's escalating campaign to achieve air supremacy over Britain. Meanwhile, some of Hitler's top advisers were urging an alternative to Sea Lion—a campaign to sweep the British from the Mediterranean and adjacent territories of North Africa and the Middle East. In the first steps of this so-called peripheral strategy, the Italians would seize the Suez Canal and the Germans would capture Gibraltar.

Hitler listened sympathetically to this proposal, but his real interests lay elsewhere: On July 31, he informed his generals that the Soviet Union must be "shattered to its roots with one blow." No action could be taken against Russia in 1940, since it was impossible to gather the necessary forces before the approach of winter. So Hitler timed the invasion, to be code-named Operation Barbarossa, for the spring of 1941. He gave several explanations for his decision, but mainly he feared the rapid growth of Soviet power. He had long regarded conflict with the Soviet Union as inevitable. In *Mein Kampf*, he had invoked the old German dream of conquest in the east. In order to fulfill that dream, he must strike at the Russians soon or the odds would turn against him.

Seasoned gambler that he was, Hitler hedged his bet by preserving his strategic options. In mid-September, he suspended Operation Sea Lion after the Luftwaffe failed in its bid to destroy the Royal Air Force, but he refused to rule out an invasion of England in the future. At the very least,

Hitler's Volatile Southern Flank

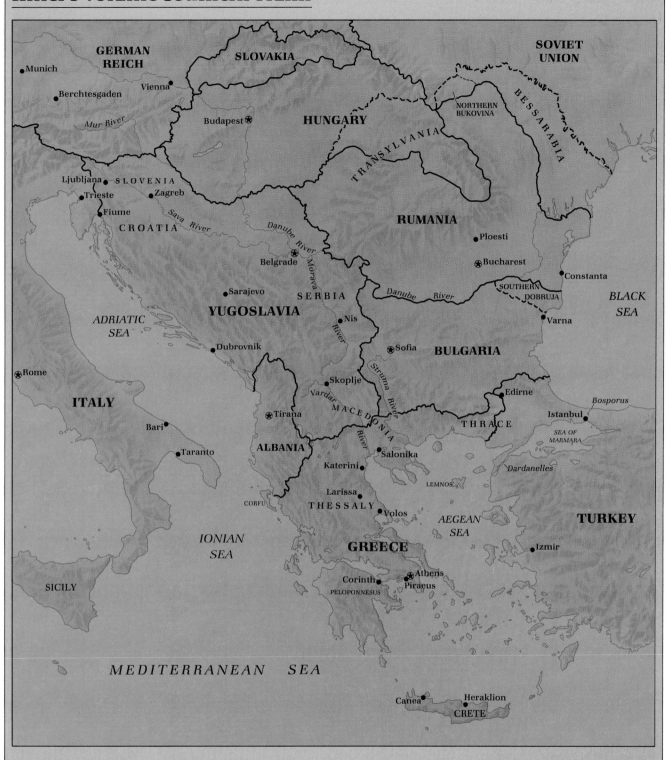

The Balkan peninsula in late 1940 was a tinderbox at the Reich's doorstep. Italy had occupied Albania the year before and was using that country as a steppingstone to invade Greece. In response, Great Britain dispatched troops to the Greek islands of Crete and Lemnos.

Rumania, meanwhile, was convulsed by the political aftershocks of territorial concessions, having yielded Bessarabia and northern Bukovina to the Soviet Union, northern Transylvania to Hungary, and southern Dobruja to Bulgaria. For their part, the Bulgarians were preoccupied

with the threat of war with Turkey to the south. Wedged between Greece and the Axis powers, Yugoslavia's situation was even more precarious. The nation was the object of fervent diplomatic pressure that fanned ethnic tensions to the point of insurrection.

planning for that contingency would serve as a screen for Barbarossa. In the meantime, Hitler ordered that the bombing of British cities continue and that preparations proceed for the assaults on Suez and Gibraltar. Increasingly, however, his attention turned to the Balkans. This area, after all, would constitute his southern flank once he launched his armies into the Soviet Union. Out of the region must come the flow of raw materials he needed to fuel his war effort. He had no immediate territorial designs on the Balkan states, but it was essential that they be both secure and responsive to the ambitions of the Third Reich.

Hitler had already forged strong links to the Balkans. Since his early days in power, he had sought to establish economic dominion over what he referred to as the "great border colonies of the European East." In doing so, he was simply conforming to a longstanding German policy of exploiting the Balkans as a source of raw materials for Germany's expanding industries. If Hitler pursued this goal more aggressively than his predecessors, it was because he was determined that Germany be independent of overseas sources of raw materials in the event of a wartime blockade.

To implement his plan, Hitler looked to the crafty Reich minister of economics, Hjalmar Schacht. Schacht's task was a difficult one, because the crushing demands of rearmament had left Germany little hard currency to offer in exchange for the resources it coveted. Instead, Schacht resorted to veiled threats, empty promises, and ingenious ploys. Beginning in 1934, he wooed the Balkan states by offering them prices for their exports well above the going rate on the world market. But payment was extended over long periods and was often made in marks that could be used only to purchase certain kinds of German manufactured goods. Thus large quantities of antiquated German weapons found their way to the Balkans while arms makers in the Reich turned out superior matériel for the Wehrmacht. Alternately, Schacht offered to work off German debts by granting the Balkan nations long-term investment credits for industrial development. But he insisted that the products turned out at the new plants be sold only to Germany. Balkan workers thus found themselves laboring for Hitler's

The German ambassador to Hungary *(left)* and the head of Hungary's national bank greet Reichsbank president Hjalmar Schacht *(center)* at the Budapest airport in 1936. Schacht's trade maneuvers shrewdly strengthened Hitler's hold on Hungary and its Balkan neighbors.

Parked behind their commander, Bulgarian soldiers in dress whites show off their German-made vehicles in 1937. Like other Balkan nations, Bulgaria exported raw materials to the Reich and imported obsolescent military equipment from Germany. The exchange furthered Hitler's rearmament program and increased the Bulgarian army's dependence on Berlin.

Reich, and the Balkan economy became increasingly an extension of Germany's own. Balkan leaders sometimes bridled at Schacht's terms, but they had nowhere else to turn: They were wary of ties to the Soviet Union, and they received few overtures from France or Britain until Germany had virtually clinched its economic hold on the region.

The Reich courted none of the Balkan states more aggressively than Rumania, prized for its vast oil deposits at Ploesti. Germany's own program to synthesize petroleum from coal was impressive, yielding three million tons a year by the late 1930s. But in wartime, the Reich would require roughly four times that amount. The deficit could be greatly reduced if the Germans controlled the Ploesti fields, which could produce seven million tons a year. In 1939, Rumania agreed to export most of its oil to Germany, frustrating a belated effort by the British to compete for the trade. In July 1940, British technicians were expelled from Ploesti at Germany's behest, a move that seemed to confirm the Allied view that Hitler had reduced Rumania to a vassal state.

The other nations on the Balkan peninsula also felt increasing pressure from the Axis that summer. Indeed, Italian troops had seized one of them, tiny Albania, in April of 1939, as Mussolini strained to keep up with the belligerent exploits of his Axis partner. Yugoslavia and Bulgaria both hoped to remain neutral but were caught in the Reich's economic web and feared Hitler's sting. Only Greece, farthest from Germany geographically, seemed intent on defying the Axis and strengthening ties with Britain—a stance that made Greece a logical target, in the duce's opinion, for his next coup.

The Balkan states might have resisted Germany's advances more successfully if they had presented a united front. But characteristically, the Balkan governments were torn between the fear of being exploited by the major powers and the desire to exploit one another. Within the region, two

Snowcapped German tank cars take on Rumanian petroleum at Ploesti during the winter of 1939-1940. The British sea blockade made control of the Ploesti fields a priority for Hitler, who told Italy's foreign minister, "I must at all costs secure the supply of oil from Rumania for carrying on the war."

generally antagonistic groupings of states had emerged when the map of Europe was redrawn at the end of World War I. On one side stood the states allied with the war's victors—Rumania, Greece, and the young nation of Yugoslavia. All three had made important territorial gains at the expense of the two vanquished states, Hungary and Bulgaria. The desire of the losers to recoup their losses and of the winners to defend their gains generated much of the tension of Balkan politics. German diplomacy in the opening stages of the Second World War strived to subtly encourage this internecine rivalry, thereby preventing the formation of a united Balkan front, and to keep the rivalries from erupting and drawing the Balkans into the war.

Above all, Hitler wanted to avoid a crisis in the region that would prompt the Soviets to dispatch troops there before the Wehrmacht was ready to invade Russia. Such thinking governed his response in June of 1940, when Russia demanded that Rumania cede the provinces of Bessarabia and northern Bukovina, whose populations were predominantly Ukrainian. Although a secret protocol to the Hitler-Stalin nonaggression pact of 1939 had recognized Russia's claim to Bessarabia, the Führer feared that these fresh Soviet demands heralded a move west that would threaten his precious oil supply. Nonetheless, he was determined to avoid a showdown in Rumania, preferring to challenge the Soviets at the time and place of his choosing. He rejected an urgent Rumanian plea for aid and left that nation with no choice but to cede the provinces.

Two months later, Hitler was again presented with a dilemma in the Balkans when Bulgaria and Hungary, inspired by Russia's example, made their own claims on Rumanian territory inhabited by their national minorities. This time, Rumania mobilized. Hitler hastily wrote a letter to the nation's monarch and dictator, King Carol II, urging him to negotiate with his belligerent neighbors. Bulgaria's comparatively modest claim was quickly settled when Rumania agreed to give up a small part of south Dobruja. But Rumania rejected Hungary's demand for Transylvania, with its one and a half million Magyars, and Hitler was forced to intervene.

The Axis governments summoned representatives of Hungary and Rumania to a meeting in Vienna. In fact, the antagonists were there not to discuss terms but to sign a settlement handed down by the German foreign minister, Joachim von Ribbentrop. His accord restored the northern third of Transylvania to Hungary but left all the region's petroleum and natural gas in Rumanian hands. Simultaneously, the Axis powers guaranteed the future territorial integrity of Rumania, a pledge that did little to soften the blow to Rumanian pride. When a map marked with Transylvania's new boundary was spread out at the conference hall, the Rumanian foreign minister fainted, fell across the table, and had to be revived with spirits.

The redrawing of Rumanian
borders in 1940 meant deliverance for some people in the
affected areas and exile for
others. Below, a German officer
overseeing the Bulgarian
occupation of southern Dobruja
accepts the thanks of peasant
women. Many residents of the
region were Bulgarian by birth.
At left, a caravan of ethnic
German refugees leaves Bessarabia across the Prut River after
the Russians seized the province.
Although Reich officials pro-
moted such emigration, they
confined the refugees to resettle-
ment camps, prompting at least
one exile to complain, "You
should have left us at home."

The Vienna Arbitration Award, as the settlement was called, not only failed to satisfy the parties concerned but set in motion events that led to the armed intervention Hitler hoped to avoid. One immediate consequence was a rapid cooling of German relations with the Russians, who correctly saw the Axis guarantee of Rumania's borders as a rebuff to Soviet ambitions in the Balkans. Another consequence was the fall of King Carol of Rumania. The Germans had never entirely trusted the king—he had a Jewish mistress and a pro-Western entourage—and felt him incapable of quelling the violent protests that followed the loss of northern Transylvania. Under German pressure, Carol abdicated the throne on September 6 in favor of his nineteen-year-old son, Michael, and transferred his powers as dictator to General Ion Antonescu, a fervent admirer of Hitler. The delighted Führer praised Antonescu for his "ruthless fanaticism," while Field Marshal Wilhelm Keitel, chief of the High Command of the Wehrmacht, extolled Antonescu's "iron determination for ruthless reform," which in this case meant reform of the Rumanian army along German lines.

Soon after Antonescu came to power, he requested the dispatch of German troops as security against the Russians. Hitler responded by sending the 13th Panzer Division and a regiment from 2d Panzer, supported by antiaircraft units and several fighter squadrons. In his secret directive

Rumania's King Carol II *(center)* **celebrates Good Friday in 1939 flanked by his son and heir, Prince Michael, and the patriarch of Bucharest. Unable to keep his pledge to yield "not a single furrow" of Rumanian soil to foreign powers, the king went into exile in September 1940.**

committing the forces, Hitler noted cynically that, "to the world, their tasks will be to guide friendly Rumania in organizing and instructing her forces." But the Führer added that their real tasks—"which must not become apparent either to the Rumanians or to our own troops"—would be to protect the oil fields and to prepare for deployment "in case a war with Soviet Russia is forced upon us."

During a visit to Rome on September 19, Ribbentrop casually mentioned to the Italian foreign minister, Galeazzo Ciano, that German "instruction units" had been sent to Rumania. But the Italian leaders did not learn how substantial those instruction units were until they read about them in the newspapers in early October. Mussolini was outraged. He forbade the Italian press to further mention the German troop movements, and he instructed Ciano to arrange for a Rumanian "request" for Italian troops to match those dispatched by Germany. Ciano in turn told the Italian ambassador in Bucharest that the request must appear "as a natural desire of Rumania even, and above all, in the eyes of the German government."

Mussolini's attempt to match Hitler's Rumanian initiative amounted to mere window dressing. In the end, Rumania received only a few officers from the Italian air force. But the duce soon decided on a far more ambitious response. On October 15, he summoned his generals to the Palazzo Venezia in Rome and told them to prepare for the invasion of Greece. He claimed that he had been pondering the move for a long time. There was some truth to this. Even before the war, he had harbored ambitions of becoming master of the Balkans. Hitler had acknowledged an Italian sphere of interest in southeastern Europe, particularly in lands bordering the Mediterranean and the Adriatic. Acting on this understanding, Mussolini had several times proposed independent Italian action against Yugoslavia or Greece but had been rebuffed by Hitler, who explained that all Axis power must be directed against England. Now the duce saw his dream of conquest threatened by the prospect of German hegemony in the Balkans.

At heart, it was a matter of prestige for Mussolini. Increasingly, he seemed not a partner in Hitler's dramatic ventures but a mere understudy, patiently awaiting each fresh German move on the world stage. Mussolini's desire to share the limelight had led him to seize Albania shortly after the Führer pounced on Czechoslovakia. Now, as Mussolini put it, he would try again to "reestablish the equilibrium." To Ciano he raged that "Hitler always faces me with a fait accompli. This time, I will pay him back in his own coin. He will discover from the newspapers that I have occupied Greece."

On reflection, Mussolini decided not to leave the matter up to the newspapers but to write Hitler instead. In his cunning letter, he ranged across a list of problems facing the Axis and only toward the end revealed

that "as regards Greece, I am resolved to put an end to the delays, and very soon." He knew as he wrote that the invasion was scheduled for four in the morning on October 28—the anniversary of his triumphant march on Rome—but he was careful not to share this detail with Hitler. He feared, noted Ciano, "that a halt order will once again arrive." The letter was dispatched to Berlin on October 23. By then, Hitler had departed for France on his special train to confer with leaders of the Vichy regime at Montoire and with General Francisco Franco at Hendaye, on the Spanish border.

Mussolini's letter was relayed to Hitler early on October 25. He did not respond immediately, perhaps because he was accustomed to the duce's boasts and bluster. Later that day, reports arrived from both the German ambassador and the Luftwaffe liaison officer in Rome recounting rumors of an imminent Italian attack. Hitler found it difficult to believe that even his inept ally would commit the folly of starting a war in the mountains of Greece in midautumn. By evening, however, he was sufficiently alarmed to order his train rerouted to Florence for consultation with Mussolini, reasoning that only a face-to-face talk with his ally could avert the danger. The train proceeded haltingly for security reasons, and by the time Hitler reached the Florence station in the morning on October 28, Italian troops had crossed the Albanian border into Greece. Hitler's ensuing conference with Mussolini was brief and seemingly cordial. But as interpreter Paul Schmidt recalled, the Führer "went north again that afternoon with bitterness in his heart."

Even as he returned to Munich from Florence, Hitler was weighing the possibility of German intervention in Greece. His worst fears about Mussolini's venture were soon realized. Far from being a "military promenade," as Ciano had promised, the Italian invasion was a disaster from the start. Torrential rains and mud bogged down the advance from Albania, and the Greeks struck back with a vengeance. Even more disturbing to Hitler was the prompt response of the British, who honored a commitment they had recently made to Greece by landing air and ground units on the islands of Crete and Lemnos a few days after the Italians had crossed the border. On November 4, Hitler convened a war council at the chancellery in Berlin, during which he denounced Mussolini's invasion as a "regrettable blunder." He pointed out that British warplanes were now within striking distance of the Rumanian oil fields and that if British troops crossed to the Greek mainland in force, Germany's entire position in the Balkans would be jeopardized. Accordingly, he directed his army chiefs to prepare for an invasion of Greece with a force of at least ten divisions.

Hitler was determined that the invasion of Russia start on schedule the

following spring and that Operation Marita, as the Greek invasion was code-named, would not interfere. It was too late to begin military operations before the onset of winter—the duce should have thought of that—but Hitler wanted his troops across the Greek frontier as soon as the snow melted in March. Final deployment orders must go out by mid-December, since the military chiefs needed two and a half months to assemble the invasion force.

The major logistical problem was how to get the troops to the Greek frontier. The direct route was via Yugoslavia. The alternate approach ran through Hungary to Rumania,

Hitler faces a deceptively genial Francisco Franco on the station platform at Hendaye on October 23, 1940. Their parley—in which the Spanish dictator avoided any commitment to enter the war against Britain—set the tone for an exasperating tour by Hitler. In Florence, he learned of Mussolini's assault on Greece.

thence across the Danube River into Bulgaria, which would become a vast staging ground for the invasion. Either plan obviously required the cooperation of the states involved. In order to secure this consent and consolidate his political hold on the Balkans, Hitler planned an intense diplomatic offensive in November.

Before dealing individually with the Balkan leaders, Hitler faced a delicate confrontation in Berlin with the Soviet foreign minister, Vyacheslav Molotov. The meeting, proposed by Ribbentrop, was an attempt to preserve at least a semblance of harmony between the two powers, whose tenuous nonaggression pact threatened to come undone at any moment. Hitler's decision to send troops to Rumania was not the only source of friction; Josef Stalin also worried that Germany might oppose his designs on neighboring Finland, and he was deeply suspicious of the recent Tripartite Pact, the military alliance between Germany, Italy, and Japan engineered by Ribbentrop in September.

Ribbentrop hoped to reduce the immediate tensions between Berlin and Moscow and perhaps achieve a lasting accord that would enable Hitler to realize his imperial ambitions without invading the Soviet Union. Ribbentrop proposed to offer Moscow the prospect of a vaguely defined sphere

Mussolini communes with his foreign minister and son-in-law, Galeazzo Ciano (center), and the German foreign minister, Joachim von Ribbentrop, at the Florence summit. An aide noted that Mussolini's confidence dissolved as the situation in Greece worsened: The duce's eyes grew "swollen and tired, his expression sad and preoccupied."

in Asia—including, perhaps, the Persian Gulf and the perimeter of the Indian Ocean—in return for a free German hand in the Balkans. Hitler, after all, had been preaching for years that Russia's traditional expansion toward central Europe and the Balkans must be deflected to the south, where it would not conflict with German interests. The breakup of the British Empire, with its vast Asian territories, might be the occasion for just such a shift in Soviet geopolitical aims. That, at least, was Ribbentrop's scheme. Hitler was skeptical. He ordered that preparations for Barbarossa continue regardless of the results of the forthcoming conference. But he was willing to see how far the Russians would bend. He scarcely reckoned that Stalin and his stubborn foreign minister expected Germany to do the yielding.

Molotov arrived in Berlin on November 12. It was a dreary, drizzly day, and the stiff reception he received from his German hosts did nothing to brighten the atmosphere. To journalist William Shirer, Molotov looked that morning like a "plugging, provincial schoolmaster." And in the conferences

Italian soldiers, their vehicles mired in mud, stand by helplessly during the Greek campaign, which bogged down because of foul weather and fierce resistance. Hitler wrote Mussolini in November pledging support but noting that the invasion might have been launched at a "more favorable time of year."

that followed, he played the role of a dour instructor, intent on destroying the pet notions of his pupils with blunt questions. He met first with Ribbentrop and brushed aside the German's claim that Britain was already beaten. Then he conferred with Hitler, who returned to the theme of London's imminent collapse and invited the Soviets in hazy terms to share in the spoils of the British Empire. That was all very well, interjected Molotov, but in the meantime, what precisely were Germany's intentions as regards Rumania? Could Hitler explain what his new order in Europe signified and how it bore on Russian interests in the Balkans and the Black Sea? Would the German leader please define the boundaries of the so-called greater Asian sphere he was offering Moscow? "The questions hailed down upon Hitler," recalled interpreter Paul Schmidt. "No foreign visitor had ever spoken to him in this way." Schmidt expected Hitler to launch into a tirade or storm out of the room, but he remained polite and controlled, only occasionally showing flashes of anger. Despite the Führer's assurances to Molotov that Britain was crumbling, the talks had to be broken off at twilight because of the danger of a night raid by British bombers.

On the second day, Ribbentrop and Hitler tried to persuade Molotov to accept a limit on Russia's territorial ambitions. To prompt him, Hitler spoke of a "purely Asiatic territory in the south that Germany already recognizes as part of the Russian sphere of interest."

Molotov, however, was not interested in generalities. Dryly, he returned to the problems of the Balkans. "You have given a guarantee to Rumania that displeases us," he said. "Is this guarantee also valid against Russia?"

"It applies to anyone who attacks Rumania," snapped Hitler.

As the discussion grew heated, Ribbentrop intervened occasionally to offer soothing words. The discussion ended inconclusively—Molotov was too experienced a campaigner to commit himself easily—and Hitler came away convinced that it was impossible to do business with the Russians.

That evening, a banquet was held at the Soviet embassy. The Führer declined to attend, leaving the task to Ribbentrop. Molotov had just proposed a toast and Ribbentrop was rising to respond when air-raid sirens announced the approach of British bombers. Ribbentrop escorted Molotov to the Foreign Ministry's excellent air-raid shelter. As the two waited for the all clear, Ribbentrop produced a draft agreement stating that Germany, Italy, Japan, and Russia respected one another's spheres of influence and would not take up arms against each other. Included was a secret protocol that defined the "territorial aspirations of the Four Countries" and assigned Russia an amorphous sphere "in the direction of the Indian Ocean." Molotov quickly made it clear that he would not be diverted into Asia so easily. He raised so many pointed questions that Ribbentrop complained

of being "queried too closely." Now that Britain had been finished, Ribbentrop added, the only important matter was whether Russia was willing to cooperate in the great liquidation of the British Empire. Molotov's retort—as Stalin repeated it a few years later to an appreciative Churchill—was yet another irksome question. If England was really finished, Molotov asked, "why are we in this shelter and whose bombs are these?"

Molotov left the next day. Word quickly went out to all German foreign missions to emphasize the friendly and constructive character of the talks. In fact, Hitler regarded them as a debacle. When the Russians finally replied to Ribbentrop's draft agreement in late November, they insisted on their continued interest in the Balkans, demanding military bases in Bulgaria as well as on the Bosporus and the Dardanelles—the straits leading from the Black Sea to the Mediterranean. Having failed to divert Russia to the south, Ribbentrop did not bother to reply. The immediate consequence of Molotov's visit was that Hitler became irrevocably committed to invading the Soviet Union. "From here, a stone started rolling," recalled his naval aide, Admiral Karl-Jesko von Puttkammer. "Hitler had firmed his decision, and no one and nothing could dissuade him."

Hitler's fresh resolve about Russia heightened his sense of urgency regarding the Balkan campaign. If he were to launch Operation Barbarossa on schedule the following spring, the conquest of Greece must be swift and sure, and that required the full cooperation of the states between the Reich and the Greek frontier. Beginning in mid-November, Hitler summoned Balkan leaders to Germany. The first visitor was King Boris III of Bulgaria, who had suspended constitutional rule in his country in the mid-1930s and now ran the state with the same domineering hand he brought to his peculiar hobby—driving locomotives. Hitler exerted all his powers of persuasion on Boris, hoping to win transit rights for German troops and Bulgarian adherence to the Tripartite Pact. As bait, Hitler offered to supply Bulgaria with a corridor to the Aegean, thus satisfying claims that Bulgaria had nursed since losing its Aegean coast to Greece in 1913.

King Boris was tempted, but he politely turned down both of Hitler's requests. One compelling reason was fear of the Soviets, who opposed Bulgarian alignment with Germany because it would impinge on their interests in the Black Sea and the Straits. Recently, Foreign Minister Molotov had bluntly informed the Bulgarian ambassador in Moscow that Russia would not tolerate Bulgaria becoming a "legionnaire state" of the Reich. The king was worried as well about provoking Turkey, which had a military alliance with Greece and a common border with Bulgaria. The Turks had concentrated thirty-seven divisions behind that border and let it be known that they would march against Bulgaria if Boris joined Mus-

solini's war on Greece. Hitler blustered that if the Turks made a move, Istanbul would suffer the fate of bomb-ruined Coventry and Birmingham, but King Boris was unconvinced. Bulgarian and Turkish diplomats were trying at that moment to avert conflict between their two countries, and the king would do nothing publicly to upset the negotiations.

With an interpreter assisting, Vyacheslav Molotov (*far left*), the Soviet foreign minister, confronts Hitler during talks begun in Berlin on November 12, 1940. A German observer noted that Molotov had the intent look of a chess player, relieved now and then by a "rather frosty smile."

Hitler nevertheless extracted one concession from his guest: Bulgaria would permit a Luftwaffe signal company, consisting of 200 men, to set up an advanced air-raid warning system along the Bulgarian-Greek border. Disguised as tourists, the men were to slip into Bulgaria in small groups. As Bulgarian concern about Soviet intentions increased, so did the number of soldier-tourists; within a few months, three companies had entered Bulgaria. These troops were crucial to Hitler's plans, because in addition to their original assignment, they built bridges, improved roads, and laid out airfields in preparation for the arrival of the main invasion force.

Hitler had far less difficulty with his next visitor, the Rumanian dictator Antonescu. Because he was partial to Antonescu, Hitler told him frankly about his plans for the invasion of Greece and about Rumania's projected role as an assembly area for German forces. Antonescu made no objection, asking only that supplies for the German troops be shipped in, since the Rumanian economy could not support them. The climax of the visit was Rumania's adherence to the Tripartite Pact on November 23. This followed by three days an identical concession by Hungary, whose leaders were so beholden to Hitler that little pressure was necessary to force them into line.

Hitler now faced the most delicate task of his diplomatic offensive as he prepared to receive a third Balkan emissary in late November—Aleksander Cincar-Marković, foreign minister of Yugoslavia. He represented a fragile constitutional monarchy that still hoped to avoid formal alignment with its Axis neighbors. Hitler was intent on winning its allegiance for a number of reasons. He could not consider his Balkan flank secure when he pushed into Russia unless he firmly held Yugoslavia, which shared a border with annexed Austria and lay close to the Ploesti oil fields. He knew also that a trunk line of the Bulgarian rail system, essential in the planning for

Bulgaria's King Boris III speaks before members of the national assembly following his meeting with Hitler in November 1940. The king's portrait dominates the chamber, flanked by those of his wife, Giovanna, and son, Simeon. The beleaguered monarch complained that "my army is pro-German, my wife is Italian, my people are pro-Russian; I alone am pro-Bulgarian."

Rumanian strongman Ion Antonescu *(left)* obliges Hitler in Berlin on November 23 by acceding to the Tripartite Pact —the military alliance binding Germany, Italy, and Japan. Antonescu's compliance paved the way for German divisions to assemble in Rumania before descending on Greece.

Operation Marita, ran within thirteen miles of the Yugoslavian frontier. Hitler's generals were uncomfortable knowing that Yugoslavia, if it mobilized, could mass more than half a million troops along that boundary. Nor would the generals be satisfied with a mere pledge of neutrality from Yugoslavia. At the very least, they wanted the Yugoslavs to grant rights of transit to the Führer's troops bound for the Bulgarian-Greek border. The rail route running from Vienna through the Yugoslavian capital of Belgrade to the Bulgarian capital of Sofia was far superior to any alternate route through Rumania; the German high command estimated that crossing Yugoslavia would shorten the buildup for Marita from ten weeks to just six—and speed the subsequent redeployment of troops for Barbarossa.

Even better from the German point of view would be a commitment from Belgrade to permit an attack on Greece from Yugoslavian territory. Yugoslavia's border with Greece offered a clearer path for an invasion than Bulgaria's, which faced the Metaxas Line, a forbidding string of Greek fortifications guarding the mountainous frontier. And an approach to Greece through Yugoslavia would be more acceptable to Turkey, since it would be farther from the Turkish border. The British were well aware of the strategic importance of Yugoslavia in German planning. It was essential, Foreign Secretary Anthony Eden wired the British ambassador in Belgrade, that Yugoslavia deny passage to German troops, "if necessary, by force."

Hitler had yet another reason for wooing the Yugoslavs. Although planning for Marita was proceeding at full steam, the Führer had a lingering hope that he could arrange a negotiated settlement of the Greek-Italian war. If the Greeks could be persuaded to expel British forces and offer a face-saving truce to Mussolini, then Germany would have achieved its aim without a costly invasion. To that end, Hitler sought to lure Yugoslavia into the Tripartite Pact by offering as bait the Greek port of Salonika, located on the Aegean near the Yugoslavian border. Belgrade longed for control of Salonika to guarantee the nation a port outside the Italian-dominated Adriatic. By taking the bait and adhering to the pact, Yugoslavia would automatically become an ally of Italy and thus potentially threaten Greece's northern frontier. Under such conditions, the Greeks would presumably be anxious to come to terms with Mussolini, even at the cost of surrendering Salonika. Hitler's hopes for this scheme had been buoyed in early November, when the Yugoslavs—concerned that Italy might yet prevail in its war on Greece and annex Salonika—instructed their military attaché in Berlin to determine "what steps might be appropriate to secure Yugoslavia's interest" in the port. But since then, the Greeks had driven the Italians back into Albania, thus weakening Hitler's hand on the eve of his meeting with the Yugoslavian foreign minister at the Führer's alpine retreat at Berchtesgaden on November 28.

To maintain secrecy, Cincar-Marković arrived at the conference by car rather than train. As the representative of a neutral state, he did not want it known that he was holding talks with Hitler. At Berchtesgaden, interpreter Schmidt noted, Hitler treated the Yugoslavian minister to "an account of his plans for the consolidation of Europe and the creation of a worldwide coalition from Yokohama to Spain." The time had come, Hitler added ominously, "when every European state had to take a stand with regard to these plans." Aside from this broad warning, however, Hitler was careful not to press Cincar-Marković too hard. He assured the minister that Germany was not insisting on anything, "not even the right of passage for troops"—knowing full well that

German generals were clamoring for that right more insistently than ever. Sensing that Cincar-Marković was not eager to sign the Tripartite Pact, Hitler spoke vaguely of a nonaggression pact between Yugoslavia, Germany, and Italy that might lead in time to a formal alliance. Cincar-Marković would promise only to refer Hitler's proposals to Belgrade for consideration. It was little indeed, but Hitler was content to let the Yugoslavs tarry, confident that events would soon force them into the fold. "The attitude of Yugoslavia is at the moment one of watchful waiting," Hitler wrote to Mussolini in December. "I do not think that any further measures on our part would be promising before the psychological situation has been generally improved once more by military successes," he added.

Yugoslavia's reluctance to align itself with the Axis powers against Greece made it all the more important for Hitler to secure an unwavering commitment from Bulgaria. As King Boris had made clear to the Führer, such a commitment would not be forthcoming so long as both Russia and Turkey stood in the way. There was little Hitler could do about the Soviets, although he felt confident that once German troops were established in Bulgaria in force, Stalin would not dare intervene.

Turkey, on the other hand, was far more susceptible to diplomatic pressure. The task of reconciling the Turks to a German presence in Bulgaria fell to Franz von Papen, the wily veteran ambassador who was expert at putting the best face on Hitler's combative designs. In late November, Papen met in Istanbul with the Turkish president, Ismet Inönü, and assured him that the Axis was quite ready to guarantee the sovereignty of his nation if only he would "cooperate in the new order in Europe." Specifically, Papen urged the president to agree to a proposed nonaggression pact that Turkish and Bulgarian diplomats had been quietly discussing for some time. The Turkish leader responded by insisting on a provision in the pact stating that the reception of any foreign troops on Bulgarian soil would be deemed a "hostile act" against Turkey. Ribbentrop, fully aware that German troops were already moving toward Bulgaria, counseled Papen to "exercise great reserve" in his dealings with the Turks until some way to pacify them could be contrived.

Near the end of January 1941, the advance elements of a German force that would grow to half a million troops started pouring into Rumania and approaching the Bulgarian border. In all, eighteen armored, infantry, and mountain divisions were to be committed. Two panzer divisions took up position in northern Dobruja, poised to race into Bulgaria in the event of an attack by Turkey. To accommodate the glut of troops, the high com-

Cartoons from a 1941 German propaganda calendar taunt British readers with the Reich's advances during 1940. Above, John Bull, tattered and seated on the rubble of London, heedlessly admires a map of Britain's blockade of Germany while U-boats hem in his own realm. At left, Rumania's accord with the Reich is signaled by a jackbooted figure kicking profiteers and Jews from the nation—a crude piece of propaganda that few outside Nazi circles would appreciate.

mand had to pressure the Rumanians into banning virtually all civilian rail traffic. Eventually, fifty trains a day were rolling across Rumania, bearing the German invasion force.

As witnesses to this buildup, the Bulgarians found themselves in an increasingly precarious position. They feared doing anything that would incite either a Russian or a Turkish reaction, yet they were clearly hostages to German power. King Boris dispatched Premier Bogdan Filov to confer first with Ribbentrop at the foreign minister's estate near Salzburg and then with Hitler at Berchtesgaden. Filov informed his hosts that Bulgaria was still unprepared to sign the Tripartite Pact but would consent to military staff talks with the Germans aimed at determining how Bulgaria could be defended against a surprise attack.

Standing with text in hand beside the seated Ribbentrop in Vienna on March 1, 1941, Premier Bogdan Filov of Bulgaria formally aligns his nation with the Axis by accepting the Tripartite Pact. Following the announcement, King Boris of Bulgaria appeared in military dress *(right, center)* to confer cordially with Field Marshal Wilhelm List *(facing the king)*, whose Twelfth Army would soon use Bulgaria as a staging area for the invasion of Greece.

Meanwhile, Papen was authorized to inform the Turks secretly that, if an incursion into Bulgaria became necessary, German troops would be ordered to remain thirty miles from the Turkish frontier. That concession was sufficient to dissolve the Turkish objection to the presence of foreign forces on Bulgarian soil. Now negotiations between Turkey and Bulgaria proceeded rapidly, and on February 17 the two countries concluded a nonaggression pact that the Nazi press hailed as a triumph of German diplomacy. On February 28, masses of German infantry—too numerous to be transported on Bulgaria's limited rail network—streamed across the Danube on pontoon bridges, while German motorized columns, hub deep in mud, started churning southward toward the Greek frontier, where the invasion was slated to begin in a month's time. On March 1, Bulgaria joined the Tripartite Pact. In return, the Germans formally promised the Bulgarians the northeastern Greek province of Thrace and, with it, access to the Aegean Sea. Hitler took the precaution of writing a conciliatory letter to President Inönü of Turkey, disclaiming any German threat to Turkish sovereignty. As for the Russians, they protested the violation of their security zone, but, as Hitler had anticipated, they did nothing to stop it.

As the last neutral in the Balkans, Yugoslavia was now under intense pressure to join the Tripartite Pact. The Yugoslavian regent, Prince Paul, and his foreign minister, Cincar-Marković, tried to placate Hitler by promising eventual adherence to the pact while naming no date. To publicly commit Yugoslavia to an alliance with Germany, they feared, would be to invite civil war in their ethnically divided nation. As regent, Prince Paul wanted to pass a united Yugoslavia to his young nephew, King Peter II. But to do so, he would somehow have to reconcile the sympathies of its dominant ethnic group, the Serbians—who had profited from Allied support in the First World War and remained staunchly anti-German—with those of the rival Croats, whose grievances were being exploited by the Axis powers. Prince Paul's dilemma was intensified by his own British sympathies—a legacy of his student days at Oxford—and by the fact that many of his leading staff officers anticipated an eventual British victory and feared the postwar consequences of an alliance with Adolf Hitler. London was doing everything it could to exploit these openings. To Churchill, Yugoslavia represented the most important center of resistance to Hitler in all

of Europe. "At this juncture," he wrote to President Franklin Roosevelt in early March, "the action of Yugoslavia is cardinal." But although the British could exhort Belgrade to resist the German tide, they could not deny that Hitler was sufficiently powerful to destroy the country of Yugoslavia if he so desired.

Aware of that reality, Prince Paul traveled secretly to Berchtesgaden two times in the month of March. Hitler was persuasive. He was asking only for a signature, he said. No German troops would pass through Yugoslavia, no territory would be demanded, no military assistance would be required. Yugoslavia, for its part, would get Salonika once the Greeks were defeated and would secure its position in the "reorganized Europe of the future." To the watching Ribbentrop, it

Poised at Bulgaria's northern frontier in early March, black-uniformed panzer crews wait for their train to proceed. Rail passage

was a luxury in backward Bulgaria; most German troops had to slog their way to the Greek border through the snow and mud.

seemed that the prince regent "was visibly impressed by these remarks."
Yet the strength of pro-British feeling in Yugoslavia, particularly in Serbian-dominated Belgrade, had impressed the prince as well. "I fear," he told
Hitler, "that if I follow your advice and sign the Tripartite Pact, I shall no
longer be here in six months." In the cafés of Belgrade, gypsy bands were
playing "Tipperary" to wild applause, and in the movie theaters, audiences
hooted and jeered when Mussolini appeared on the newsreel screen. The
Yugoslavian ambassador in Washington sent an impassioned telegram to
Prince Paul, begging him not to give in to Hitler.

As word began to circulate in mid-March that the prince and his ministers were on the verge of yielding to German pressure, angry letters and
telegrams flooded the offices of Yugoslavian cabinet members and military
leaders. Amid threats on Prince Paul's life, delegations arrived in the capital
to protest the anticipated move. Yugoslavian diplomats overseas threatened resignation, and the crews of Yugoslavian ships docked in foreign
ports voted to remain in exile. Two appeals came from London—one from
King George VI addressed to the regent and the other from Churchill to
Prime Minister Dragiša Cvetković. If Yugoslavia were to "become an ac-
complice in an attempted assassination of Greece," warned Churchill, "her
ruin will be certain and irrevocable." In a secret telegram, he told the British
ambassador, Ronald Campbell, to "pester, nag, and bite" and to neglect no
"alternative" to keep Yugoslavia out of the Axis fold. Churchill's exhorta-
tions were matched by those of President Roosevelt, but neither leader
could offer the Yugoslavs more than vague promises of aid when and if the
tide of the war turned.

On March 20, Prince Paul announced to the cabinet that Yugoslavia
would sign the Tripartite Pact. In a tense meeting with the American
ambassador, Arthur Bliss Lane, he explained that he had no choice. If
Belgrade spurned the Germans, it could not count on the support of the
Croats in the invasion that would inevitably follow. The nation had few
arms, Paul added, and most of what it had came from Germany. When Lane
spoke of Yugoslavia's honor, the prince cut him short. "You big nations are
hard," he said. "You talk of our honor, but you are far away." When Lane
saw the prince again on March 23, Paul was distraught. The Germans had
given him until midnight to tell them when Yugoslavian delegates would
be arriving in Vienna "to conclude the agreements prepared." Some of the
regent's closest advisers were still warning that to sign would spark "revolution in the country and insurrection in the army." He made no secret
of his distress: "I am out of my head."

The next morning, Prime Minister Cvetković and Foreign Minister
Cincar-Marković left for Vienna to sign the Tripartite Pact. Their hour of

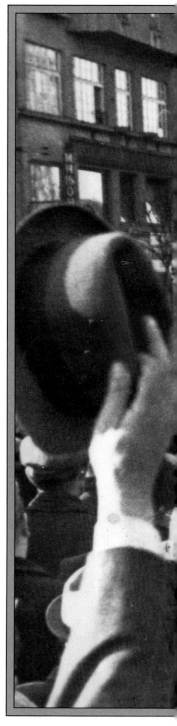

Celebrating the coup d'état
staged by Yugoslavian officers
opposed to an alliance with
Germany, Serbians wave their
national banner in the streets of
Belgrade. The uprising incensed
Hitler, who decreed that even if
the rebels relented and offered
Berlin "declarations of loyalty,"
Yugoslavia was to be "destroyed
as quickly as possible."

Attired as commander in chief, King Peter II of Yugoslavia inspects his palace guard in Belgrade on March 28, 1941. General Dušan Simović (*second from left*), leader of the anti-Nazi coup, accompanies him. Fearing retribution, Simović had the king taken each night from the palace to an air-raid shelter.

departure was not announced for fear of hostile demonstrations. Hitler received them cordially, complimented them on Yugoslavia's wise decision, and promised always to be a loyal friend. As they were leaving, he asked them to convey his best wishes to Prince Paul.

The two ministers returned on March 26 to a country that was ominously calm. That evening, officers in the Yugoslavian army and air force launched a lightning coup that toppled the government before the night was over. Troops from Belgrade's central air-force base fanned out across the city to seize the ministry of war, the police headquarters, the main post office and telephone exchanges, and the radio station. So widespread was the sentiment of revolt that when two rebel battalions marched to the royal palace, the palace guard opened the gates and joined the uprising without firing a shot. Cvetković was arrested at his suburban villa. Prince Paul, who was traveling by train to his estate in the north of the country, was intercepted at Zagreb and brought back to the capital, where he resigned as regent, leaving the young King Peter to rule at the rebels' behest.

The coup touched off scenes of wild celebration in Belgrade. Jubilant citizens flew handmade British, American, and French flags from lampposts, chanted the national anthems of Britain and Yugoslavia, and paraded pictures of Roosevelt and Churchill through the streets. In London, Churchill told a cheering House of Commons that "Yugoslavia has found her soul." The delirium was short-lived, however, once the leaders of the overnight coup took stock of their situation in the harsh light of day. To be sure, the British welcomed the uprising—they may even have abetted it—but they were in no position to defend the rebels against a German onslaught. On March 30, the new government announced that it would remain faithful to the Tripartite Pact.

The rebels thus adopted the very policy that had caused them to revolt. Unfortunately, their overtures to Hitler came too late. To the Führer—who considered any agreement he made sacrosanct until he himself was ready to violate it—the Belgrade coup was a gross provocation. He immediately ordered an invasion "to smash Yugoslavia militarily and as a state." To all around him he raged that "there must never again be a Yugoslavia." The new regime's subsequent pledge of cooperation did not mollify Hitler, who feared that the rebels might still cast their lot with the British. Accordingly, the invasion of Greece from Bulgaria was postponed while his chiefs hastily drafted plans for a simultaneous assault on Yugoslavia. On April 2, Ribbentrop informed officials at the German embassy in Belgrade that upon receiving the code words "Tripartite Pact," they were to destroy all files and leave the city as soon as possible. At four in the morning on April 6, the code was issued. Belgrade's nightmare was about to begin. ✠

A Staunch New Ally for the Reich

As Hitler wooed the Balkan states in the autumn of 1940, he found no nation more receptive to his overtures than Rumania. Its new leader, General Ion Antonescu, was an ardent admirer of the Führer. And when Antonescu assumed power following the abdication of King Carol II in September of 1940, he formed a government in partnership with a paramilitary organization, the Iron Guard, that was fiercely pro-Nazi. For more than a decade, the legionnaires of the Iron Guard had been clamoring for a formal alliance with the Nazis, and now they would have their wish.

Antonescu styled his new government the Legionary State and named the Iron Guard its sole legitimate party. Emboldened by their official status, the legionnaires embarked on a Nazi-like orgy of terror, murdering Jews and political opponents by the score. The convulsive civil disorder proved too much even for Hitler, whose pressing need for a stable and productive Rumania overshadowed his approval of the legionnaires' goals. With the Führer's blessing, Antonescu dismantled the Legionary State in February 1941 and installed a new military government.

The Rumanian strongman soon became one of Hitler's favorite allies, virtually the only person ever allowed to contradict the Führer. Antonescu was also the only Axis partner whose military advice was ever seriously solicited and the first foreigner to be decorated with the coveted Knight's Cross of the Iron Cross. His anti-Semitism rivaled Hitler's own: During the Rumanian's four-year rule, 270,000 of the country's 757,000 Jews were exterminated.

Under Antonescu's leadership, Rumania would prove to be Germany's most loyal and valuable Axis partner, supplying oil to fuel the German war machine, opening its strategically placed territories to German troops as a staging ground for the invasions of Yugoslavia, Greece, and Russia, and ultimately joining the Reich in battle against the Soviet Union.

Marching through Bucharest in a parade celebrating the formation of a new government in September 1940, young Iron Guard legionnaires dressed in Rumanian peasant garb give a stiff-armed fascist salute to head of state Ion Antonescu *(standing next to the Nazi banner)*. Above the reviewing stand hangs a portrait of the xenophobic Iron Guard founder, Corneliu Codreanu, who had been assassinated in 1938 at the behest of King Carol II.

Luftwaffe airmen brief a leather-helmeted Rumanian trainee on the technique of piloting the Henschel 126, a German reconnaissance plane. Ostensibly, German units came to Rumania to teach modern military tactics to members of the Rumanian officer corps—previously noted more for their uniforms than their fighting ability. In fact, the Rumanian-based German troops—more than half a million strong by early 1941—were there to secure Rumania's oil fields and to prepare for the invasions of the Balkans and Russia.

In a drill early in 1941, a Luftwaffe flak crew races to man a
20-mm antiaircraft gun in a reinforced pit on the perimeter of
the Ploesti oil fields of eastern
Rumania. Protecting Ploesti from
Greek-based British bombers
was a top priority for Hitler, who
described the threat to the refin-
eries as "positively terrifying."

The headquarters unit of a German panzer division—part of an eight-division invasion force en route to Greece—crosses the Danube, leaving Rumania and entering Bulgaria on the morning of March 1, 1941. That day, Bulgaria signed the Tripartite Pact and, like Rumania, officially cast its lot with the Germans.

TWO

A Punitive Blitzkrieg

A German tank crew maneuvers around a concrete barrier near the Yugoslavian border during the offensive that began on April 6, 1941. Striking before the Yugoslavs were fully mobilized, armored spearheads burst through such fortified points and raced toward the capital, Belgrade, which was already being devastated by the Luftwaffe.

The day dawned quietly in Belgrade. But those who were awake at first light on this Sunday morning, April 6, 1941, felt the tension in the air. Ruth Mitchell, an American-born photographer who had lived in the Yugoslavian capital for more than a year, was eating breakfast in the sitting room of her home on Slavija Hill, south of the Danube. "Outside my windows," she wrote, "the dark-browed Serbian peasants, the men in somber dark, the women in their bright embroidered clothes, passed unhurriedly but more silently, more grimly than usual to the early Sunday market. I watched them thoughtfully as I began to pour my tea and turned the short-wave radio knob." Suddenly, a strident German voice accosted her over the radio speaker. It was Hitler's foreign minister, Joachim von Ribbentrop, informing the public of the Führer's decision to punish the "clique of conspirators in Belgrade" and to restore "peace and security" in Yugoslavia by force of arms. Ribbentrop announced that bombs were already raining down on Belgrade, a claim that proved premature. Mitchell could hear "no sound but the jingling of milk carts in the streets and the shuffling of peasant feet. But it was coming, this raucously heralded doom."

Within minutes, she detected the first dull explosions in the distance and the whine of approaching dive bombers. Taking shelter beneath the stairs with her cook, Mitchell endured blast after blast, some within thirty yards of her home. "The effect was almost inconceivable," she wrote. "It wasn't the noise or even so much the concussion; it was the perfectly appalling wind that was most terrifying. It drove like something solid through the house. Every door that was latched simply burst off its hinges, every pane of glass flew into splinters. The curtains stood straight out into the room and fell back in ribbons." After the thunderous shocks came a quieter but no less disturbing noise: "With a weird, smooth sound like the tearing of silk, the neighboring houses began to collapse."

Unlike many of her neighbors, Mitchell survived unscathed. The air raid she had experienced was the opening sortie in the Luftwaffe's aptly named Operation Punishment, designed to paralyze the Yugoslavian government by devastating the capital. In the first wave of this assault alone, more than

330 warplanes—74 dive bombers, 160 medium bombers, and 100 fighters—made Belgrade their target. By contrast, the Yugoslavian Royal Air Force had only about 340 warplanes dispersed across the entire country. And by the time the first alarms sounded in Belgrade around a quarter of seven, preemptive strikes against the nation's main air bases had already put a number of the Yugoslavian planes out of action. Those Yugoslavian fighter pilots who made it into the air to challenge the onslaught were far less experienced than their German counterparts. Ironically, many were flying the same craft as their Luftwaffe opponents—Messerschmitts obtained from Germany before relations between the two countries soured—and thus were subject to friendly fire from Yugoslavian antiaircraft batteries. Of the ten Me 109s in one Yugoslavian squadron assigned to protect the capital, half were disabled or destroyed in the first raid.

Such damage left the defenders in no position to cope with the succeeding air strikes on Belgrade, which came at intervals of two to four hours in waves of 150 planes each. One Yugoslavian lieutenant, who was flying an Me 109 at high altitude that afternoon, was stunned by the sight of the German aerial armada arrayed beneath him. "I never saw so many aircraft together in my life, not even in a photo or in the cinema." Steeling himself, the lieutenant latched onto a trailing Luftwaffe bomber and dispatched it with a burst from his nose-mounted 7.9-mm guns. But such isolated victories did little to protect Belgrade. Swooping down with awesome precision, the Luftwaffe's dive bombers destroyed government buildings and communications facilities in the capital and bombed army headquarters, inflicting crippling casualties on the army high command. All communication with the Yugoslavian field armies was severed. Medium bombers, meanwhile, carpeted residential areas with explosives. Many people died in their shattered houses or tenements; others were entombed in the city's inadequate air-raid shelters. Ruth Mitchell, who fled the city during a lull in the bombing that Sunday, happened upon one shelter that had received a direct hit. All that was left of the refuge was a gaping hole, surrounded by uprooted trees. Their branches were littered with "parts of human bodies, arms, legs, heads."

To compound the carnage, the Luftwaffe dropped mostly incendiaries on Belgrade in the afternoon, setting off towering fires that would guide the raiders who came that night. From her refuge north of the Danube, Mitchell looked back that evening to witness a city that "seemed to be one blazing bonfire. Great tongues of flame would burst up suddenly, glare fiercely for a while, and slowly sink away. Germany had lit the great beacon of her 'civilizing mission' in the Balkans."

The assault on Belgrade continued for two days, killing 17,000 and

Striking Yugoslavia from All Sides

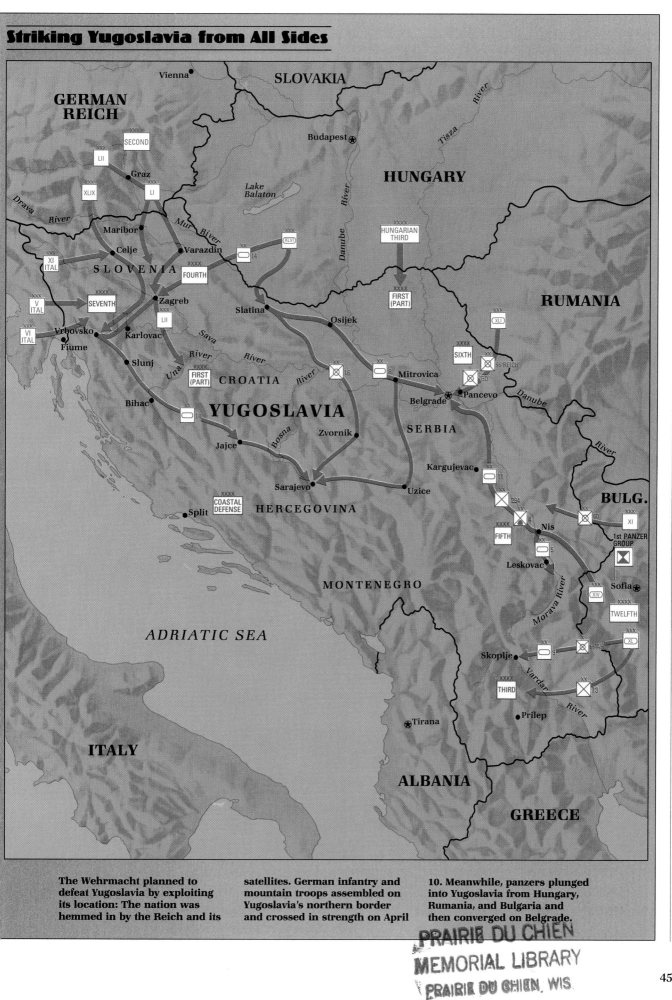

The Wehrmacht planned to defeat Yugoslavia by exploiting its location: The nation was hemmed in by the Reich and its satellites. German infantry and mountain troops assembled on Yugoslavia's northern border and crossed in strength on April 10. Meanwhile, panzers plunged into Yugoslavia from Hungary, Rumania, and Bulgaria and then converged on Belgrade.

wounding more than 50,000. Its ferocity sobered even some who were close to Hitler and normally endorsed his punitive tactics. "Horrifying reports of the air raid on Belgrade," Propaganda Minister Joseph Goebbels noted in his diary on April 7. But he professed no sympathy for a people whose leaders had dared to defy Hitler, however briefly: "This is the punishment they have earned." If any of the Führer's military advisers harbored qualms about the operation, they had little time to ponder them, because the Wehrmacht had embarked on a campaign of staggering complexity.

Hitler's last-minute decision to subjugate Yugoslavia transformed his original Balkan plan, which had called for the invasion of only Greece. Now the Wehrmacht would have to deploy its forces to attack Yugoslavia and Greece simultaneously in order to avoid a prolonged Balkan campaign that might significantly delay the forthcoming invasion of Russia. The additional burden produced a tactical advantage for the Greek operation, however. No longer would the German generals be restricted to a frontal assault on the formidable Metaxas Line along the Bulgarian-Greek frontier. They could now exploit the pathways into Greece that they had coveted from the start: the lightly defended passes along the Yugoslavian-Greek frontier. Within twenty-four hours of Hitler's decision, the German high command had drawn up a plan that called for part of Field Marshal Wilhelm List's Twelfth Army, massed in southern Bulgaria, to attack the Metaxas Line as planned while mechanized units drove westward into Yugoslavia and then swung south into Greece. This flanking movement was designed to drive a wedge between the defenders of the Metaxas Line in the east and the bulk of the Greek army, which was committed against the Italians in Albania. One obstacle might block the attackers' path—a recently arrived expeditionary force of some 54,000 British and Commonwealth troops, including one Australian and one New Zealand division and a British armored brigade. But the German high command felt confident that List's army was equal to the challenge.

The hastily improvised assault on Yugoslavia, meanwhile, would continue to test the Wehrmacht's flexibility. It was not enough to simply pulverize Belgrade; as the Germans had learned in the Battle of Britain, punishing enemies from the air could not guarantee their surrender. Yugoslavia would have to be conquered by German troops, and that meant a massive redeployment of far-flung Wehrmacht forces in a matter of days. The vital task of forcing Yugoslavia's northern frontier was assigned to General Maximilian von Weichs's Second Army. But when Weichs received his orders in late March, his would-be invasion force was scattered all over Europe. He and his staff had their headquarters in Munich; many of his units were stationed in France; his 14th Panzer Division had recently been

Flames engulf outmoded Yugoslavian fighters at an airstrip near Belgrade on April 6, after a German air raid. Information furnished by a Yugoslavian defector helped the Luftwaffe pinpoint many small airfields across the country. By day's end, the Luftwaffe had damaged or destroyed more than one-fourth of Yugoslavia's warplanes.

posted to the Russian border to prepare for the invasion there. Hurriedly, that division pulled up stakes and lumbered by road and rail to the Hungarian-Yugoslavian frontier, where it joined the 8th Panzer and 16th Motorized Infantry Divisions from France to form the XLVI Panzer Corps under General Heinrich von Vietinghoff. Most of Vietinghoff's corps was slated to descend on Belgrade from the north as part of a three-pronged assault on the capital. General Georg-Hans Reinhardt's independent XLI Panzer Corps would drive westward from Rumania, and General Ewald von Kleist's panzer group—detached from the Twelfth Army—would move north from Bulgaria. Meanwhile, the infantry and mountain troops that formed the bulk of Weichs's Second Army would assemble in Austria (now

part of the Reich), cross the mountainous frontier into Yugoslavia, capture the city of Zagreb, and secure the nation's rugged western frontier.

Many of the units assigned to the operation were still a few days from their staging areas on April 6, when the Luftwaffe launched Operation Punishment and the Twelfth Army began its concerted drive in the south. But the elements that had reached Yugoslavia's northern frontier were in no mood that morning to wait idly for their comrades when they saw a chance to take the initiative. A few units had already seized bridges along the border to keep the Yugoslavs from destroying them. Now German troops—some acting on orders and others on their own authority—began to probe enemy territory.

Among those to lead the way were members of a special assault force code-named *Feuerzauber*, or Magic Fire, whose mission was to secure critical points along the Reich-Yugoslavian border until the Second Army was ready to launch its main drive. One such unit, commanded by a Captain Palten, took hold of a vital frontier bridge over the Mur River as ordered. Then Palten and his troops grew impatient. The route across the bridge led south to the Yugoslavian town of Maribor, ten miles away, and thence to Zagreb. Before dawn on April 6, Palten's men advanced without authorization southward into Yugoslavian territory in order to secure the high ground there. The attacks proved so successful that Palten was encouraged to lead an impromptu raid on Maribor two days later. Encountering little opposition, his men filed south between snowcapped peaks, crossed a stream north of Maribor on inflated rafts, and took possession of the town by nightfall.

Palten's superiors were not about to reward him for this feat. Regular infantry units took over in Maribor, and Palten and his raiders were recalled to the northern border, where they spent the rest of the campaign ignominiously patrolling the frontier. But the exploit offered vivid proof of how easily Yugoslavian territory could be penetrated. In another advance, a German bicycle detachment, part of the 183d Infantry Regiment, pedaled into the town of Murska Sobota, northeast of Maribor, and claimed it for the Reich without firing a shot.

Where Yugoslav resistance materialized, it soon melted away. One German *Gebirgsjäger*, or alpine infantry, company that occupied an isolated village south of the border was surprised in the night by Yugoslavian soldiers who burst out of the woods, firing wildly and heaving hand grenades. Most of the Germans were billeted in houses at the edge of the village and had to fumble in the dark for their weapons and gear as the windows shattered around them. As one of the men in the company recalled, several bleary-eyed machine gunners rushed out to engage the

Undeterred by a broken bridge, troops of the LI Infantry Corps advancing toward Zagreb jury-rig a precarious span over the roiling Drava River on April 10. Elsewhere in the region, demoralized Yugoslavian troops abandoned vital bridges intact.

enemy "dressed only in their underclothes, boots, and helmets." Nonetheless, their response was persuasive. Soon the disorganized attack faltered, and the Yugoslavs "vanished into the trees, leaving behind their dead and wounded as well as some equipment."

The sorry state of the Yugoslavian defenses in the north reflected the central government's tenuous hold on the region. Troops stationed there could count on little support either from the area's Croatian majority—which was hostile to Serbian rule in Belgrade and hoped for something better from the Axis—or from the many ethnic Germans concentrated near the country's border with the Reich. One Austrian-born soldier who crossed with the German vanguard into Yugoslavia relished the welcome he received from townspeople who shared his language and culture. "When we first entered the towns, we were greeted as liberators with flowers and wine," he recalled, "and for the first days it was just like a maneuver—a battle of flowers."

Moreover, the German sympathizers were not confined to the civilian population. The Yugoslavian Fourth Army, which was responsible for the defense of the Hungarian border, included a large number of Croats, who needed little incentive to turn against their government. On April 6, advance elements of Vietinghoff's XLVI Panzer Corps provided them with an opportunity by establishing bridgeheads across the Mur and Drava rivers. Sensing a rout in the offing, Croatian soldiers mutinied at several points along the line, turning an already-precarious situation for the defenders into a desperate ordeal.

Thus the Germans did much to demoralize the Yugoslavs in the opening days of the campaign, while the bulk of the invasion force was still moving into line. By evening on April 9, Weichs's Second Army was ready to bring its full weight to bear against a tottering foe. At dawn the next day, infantry and armored divisions surged across the border and hastened toward their objectives. In the Maribor sector, most of the Yugoslavian Seventh Army had already withdrawn toward Zagreb, leaving behind only a thin screen of troops to cover the retreat. On learning of the situation from air reconnaissance, Weichs ordered his LI Infantry Corps to send motorized units ahead in pursuit. These flying columns had to contend with blinding snowsqualls in the high passes and flooded streams in the valleys. But by the afternoon of April 11, Weichs's vanguard was approaching Zagreb. Far from resisting the German tide, authorities there proclaimed an independent Croatian state and called on civilians and soldiers alike to cease all hostile acts against the occupiers.

To the east, meanwhile, the three prongs of the German panzer assault on Belgrade were nearing their objective. The tank crews of Vietinghoff's

A German motorcycle reconnaissance unit entering the city of Zagreb runs a festive gauntlet of welcoming Croats. Opposition to Serbian domination in Yugoslavia led many Croats to hail the invaders as liberators.

XLVI Corps had rumbled across their bridgeheads from Hungary early on April 10 and encountered virtually no opposition from the crumbling Fourth Army as they drove south. In the early-morning hours of April 12, the 8th Panzer Division reached the Sava River, forty miles to the west of Belgrade. Reinhardt's XLI Corps was even closer to its goal that night; it had advanced from the Rumanian border to the city of Pancevo, on the Danube, a mere twelve miles northeast of the Yugoslavian capital. The third prong in the German attack—Kleist's panzer group—was still more than forty miles southeast of the target after a grueling march. Their long route from the Bulgarian border had taken them through the heart of Serbia, where resistance to the intruders was stiffest.

Aware of the challenges that lay before Kleist's force, the high command had sent it across the frontier at dawn on April 8, two days before the all-out

Elements of the 11th Panzer Division roll through Nis on April 9, churning past a blazing truck in an abandoned Yugoslavian

convoy. The division, leading General Ewald von Kleist's panzer group, covered the remaining 140 miles to Belgrade in four days.

invasion of Yugoslavia. Supported by powerful artillery and frequent air strikes by the Luftwaffe, Kleist's armor broke through a strong line of bunkers and antitank batteries held by the determined Serbians of the Yugoslavian Fifth Army. Forging ahead through a steep mountain pass, the German vanguard captured the city of Nis on April 9, leaving behind dirt roads that were so rutted by tank tracks that yoked oxen had to haul the trailing German supply vehicles up the steep pass. By April 10, Kleist's panzers were driving northwestward from Nis through the Morava Valley to Belgrade, encountering pockets of fierce resistance along the way. At Kragujevac, the location of a major arms plant, the courageous director of the arsenal responded to the approach of German tanks by handing out weapons to thousands of employees. Some discarded their arms before the Germans entered the town, but others used them in a guerrilla war that began in earnest that summer and prompted harsh reprisals by the oc-cupiers. Ultimately, partisans would cause the Germans far more trouble in Yugoslavia than did the Yugoslavian armies.

Waffen-SS troops in camouflage uniforms cross the broad Danube River to Belgrade as German forces close on the Yugoslavian capital. SS Captain Fritz Klingenberg (*inset*) led the first detachment to reach Belgrade and claimed the city with a handful of men on April 12. For his feat, Klingenberg received the Knight's Cross.

As Kleist's panzers drew closer to Belgrade, they found villages fortified like the French towns that German soldiers had encountered the year before. The small town of Natalinci, for instance, was one extended tank trap, fronted by deep ditches and downed trees and defended by an artillery battery directed from an observation post in the church tower. Kleist's tank commanders had learned their lessons well on the western front, however. Refusing to be drawn into protracted struggles, they sent the lead tanks in to keep the defenders busy, while succeeding units swung around the strongpoints and rolled on toward the capital. Supporting infantry units moved in to secure the towns.

As it happened, the honor of claiming the capital fell to SS Captain Fritz Klingenberg and members of his motorcycle assault company, a unit of the motorized SS division Reich, part of Reinhardt's corps attacking from Rumania. On the morning of April 12, Klingenberg and his vanguard approached Belgrade from Pancevo along the north bank of the Danube River. The prospect that lay before them was less than inviting. The flood-swollen river separated them from the ravaged capital. The bridge they had hoped to use—purposely spared by the Luftwaffe in its opening bombardment—had been blown up by the enemy. And they carried no rafts or bridging equipment. Still, the prize was within sight, and Klingenberg was determined to try for it. His men located a motorboat on the north bank, and in midafternoon the captain pushed off for the capital with one of his platoon leaders, two sergeants, and five privates. They were nearly swamped when the surging current forced the boat against a pier of the wrecked bridge, but they worked the craft free and reached the far shore. Klingenberg sent two men back in the boat to fetch reinforcements, then turned his mind to the task at hand—capturing an enemy capital with only a small number of soldiers.

Two factors worked in Klingenberg's favor: the confusion wrought by the recent bombing of the city and the element of surprise—the capital was bracing for a massive onslaught, not a furtive raid. Soon after Klingenberg landed, his tiny task force encountered a contingent of twenty Yugoslavian soldiers. Stunned by the unheralded arrival of the enemy in their midst, the Yugoslavs surrendered without a fight. A short time later, a few military vehicles approached the raiders. With a brief burst of fire, Klingenberg's men took possession of the carriers. Aided by an ethnic German who volunteered to serve as guide and interpreter, Klingenberg set out with his freshly motorized unit for the Yugoslavian war ministry. It was a hellish journey past smoldering barracks and bombed-out tenements cloaked with the stench of death. The men reached the ministry and found it an empty shell. No high command remained in Belgrade to be reckoned with.

Klingenberg then drove to the German legation, where he was met enthusiastically by the military attaché, who had remained in the city through the bombardment. At five o'clock, the Germans unfurled a swastika and ran it up the building's bare flagpole to proclaim the capture of the capital. Two hours later, the mayor of Belgrade appeared at the legation with other local officials to formally surrender. It was not until dawn on April 13 that panzers entered the city in force to back up Klingenberg's bluff.

The captain's audacious feat characterized the German campaign in Yugoslavia as a whole. From beginning to end, the invasion was more a masterful exercise in intimidation than an armed struggle. When the vestiges of the Yugoslavian government conceded defeat on April 17—two days after the fall of Sarajevo had eliminated the last bastion of official resistance—the Wehrmacht could congratulate itself on having overrun a nation roughly the size of England at a cost of only 558 German casualties, including 151 killed. But neither Hitler nor his generals were prepared to celebrate yet. At the southern tip of the Balkan peninsula, a more strenuous and significant contest was still raging.

Unlike the sprawling ground attack on Yugoslavia, which began with isolated shocks and tremors, the battle for Greece erupted at dawn on April 6 with the concentrated fury of a volcano. From their rugged staging ground in southwestern Bulgaria, forces of the German Twelfth Army burst out in several directions. The swiftest encroachments were made to the west, as panzers began their flanking movement along two routes, one cutting across the southeastern tip of Yugoslavia to the Vardar Valley and thence to the vital Greek port of Salonika, and the other passing through the Yugoslavian city of Skoplje to the Monastir Gap and central Greece. Simultaneously, the superbly trained alpine infantry divisions of Lieut. General Franz Böhme's XVIII Mountain Corps launched frontal assaults on the Metaxas Line, the forbidding complex of bunkers and fieldworks that extended eastward from the Vardar Valley along the steep ridge separating Macedonian Greece from Bulgaria.

Among the agile alpine troops testing the Metaxas Line were the men of Brigadier General Julius Ringel's 5th Mountain Division, assigned to smash through the cordon at one of its most powerful points, just west of the Struma River. Ringel's soldiers proudly referred to themselves as mountain goats. They had earned that label in the days preceding the attack by carting ammunition surefootedly up winding paths from the Bulgarian border town of Petrich to their forward positions, sequestered in the wooded slopes below the enemy line. Amid the grueling preparations, the Germans were treated to bracing vistas—high peaks mantled in snow,

meadows sprinkled with crocuses, and distant valleys covered with almond and fig trees in first bloom. But as night fell on the eve of the battle,
there was little to distract the men from the grim prospect ahead. For many,
it was their first test in combat, and they slept little as an icy wind whistled
through the branches overhead. Some felt their stomachs churning with
fear; others were consumed by hunger. One hulking engineer dipped into
his emergency rations in the middle of the night and opened some tinned
meat. "Who knows when I'll be picked off," he explained to his mates. "It
would be a pity for this stuff to go to waste."

By five in the morning on April 6, the troops were poised for the assault.
They had strapped their rifles across their chests, and the other instru-
ments of their trade—wire cutters, flare guns, entrenching tools, hand
grenades—hung from their belts. A short time later, German antitank and
field guns opened up on the Greek strongholds above, and the reports
echoed through the gorges that separated the fortified peaks. Moments of
eerie silence, broken only by the twittering of birds in the dawn light,
followed the opening bombardment. Then shriller notes filled the air as
flights of Stukas approached to pound the enemy positions, raising clouds
of grit that shrouded the mountaintops in a lingering ocher haze. While the
bombs were still falling, the soldiers left the cover of the woods and
scrambled up snowy slopes that the Greeks had cleared of timber to
provide their gunners with unobstructed fields of fire. Withering fire met
the attackers as they neared the bunkers—proof that the thick concrete-
and-steel shelters had largely withstood the aerial barrage. The Germans
would have to take the redoubt by storm.

Over the next few hours, the mountain troops gouged holes in the Greek
line by ousting enemy troops from some of the trenches that flanked the
bunkers. The engineers blasted some of the casemates open with explosives or scorched the Greek gunners with flamethrowers aimed through
the embrasures. Around midday, other Greeks responded by calling in
artillery fire on their own positions—killing and wounding scores of Germans but doing little harm to themselves. Exposed on the slopes, mountain
troops huddled in the abandoned Greek trenches or burrowed into shell
craters for protection. Through the afternoon and evening, Greek soldiers
emerged sporadically from their coverts in an effort to drive the Germans
from the positions they had seized. But the men of the 5th Mountain clung
to their toeholds on the Metaxas Line. Bolstered by reinforcements in the
night, they attacked with renewed determination at dawn. Grappling up
cliffs made slick by freezing rain, they blasted or burned the Greeks from
one bunker after another. By evening on April 7, Germans were pouring
through wide gaps in the line and heading across the plain to the south.

Rugged Gear for the Alpine Elite

The soldiers of the German mountain divisions that stormed the icy, wind-swept Metaxas Line had cause to be thankful for their special clothing and equipment. Along with a water-resistant jacket *(below, right)*, they wore a wool tunic, thick, ski-style trousers, and cleated climbing boots. Woolen puttees prevented snow from sifting into the men's low-cut boots.

Officers were outfitted with essentially the same clothing, plus a service tunic *(below, left)* with light green piping on the insignia. When not wearing a steel helmet, all ranks wore a mountain cap *(far left)*, a World War I design with a fold-down ear-and-neck flap.

A mountain soldier's rucksack *(below)* held spare clothing, personal effects, high-energy rations, and climbing gear, such as pitons, lace-on crampons, ski-repair kits, a poncho that doubled as a shelter half, and lightweight climbing rope. The ice ax served as an alpenstock, or hiking stick.

The enameled *Bergführer-abzeichen*, or mountain leader's badge *(top)*, authorized in 1936, was awarded to officers and enlisted men of good character and leadership ability who passed a rigorous alpine training course and served at least a year as qualified mountain troops. All mountain personnel wore the badge above—an edelweiss ringed by entwined climbing rope—on their right sleeve.

The savage contest cost the division 160 lives—or nine more than the Wehrmacht had lost in the entire campaign for Yugoslavia.

Meanwhile, the 6th Mountain Division, attacking to the right of the 5th, was scoring a coup of its own. The troops climbed through deep snow to a stretch of the Metaxas Line so remote and high—7,000 feet—that the Greeks considered it inaccessible. There the Germans pushed through the lightly defended position and marched down the south side of the ridge, reaching the rail line to Salonika east of Lake Dojran late on April 7. The mountain troops were still a long way from the port, however. A German contingent better equipped for the task—the armored vanguard of the 2d Panzer, a division that had been attached to General Böhme's corps—would, in fact, capture the city.

The panzers' swift descent into Greece bore little resemblance to the slogging advance of the infantrymen. In a deft end run around the Metaxas Line, the 2d Division motored west to the Yugoslavian town of Strumica on April 6, encountering little resistance along the way. The panzers then turned south toward the Greek border. Obsessed with the threat from their traditional rivals, the Bulgarians, the Greeks had done little to fortify their frontier with Yugoslavia, and the panzers surged across easily. Brushing aside a Greek motorized infantry division near Lake Dojran, the German armored columns descended on Salonika, claiming the city without a fight on the morning of April 9. The division's drive to the sea spelled doom for the Greek Second Army, which had taken a beating along the Metaxas Line and was now cut off. That same day, the commander of the Second Army surrendered unconditionally.

Another crushing blow was about to fall on the Greeks and their British allies. At the north end of the Monastir Gap—the strategic corridor from Yugoslavia to central Greece—General Georg Stumme was preparing to launch the lead elements of his XL Panzer Corps across the frontier on April 10. Stumme's panzers had been assigned the broader of the two flanking movements through southern Yugoslavia, a path that had taken them west from Bulgaria to the city of Skoplje, which they captured on April 7. Then they drove south through the towns of Prilep and Bitolj to the Greek border. Their swift advance gravely threatened the Greek First Army in Albania. Reluctant to yield ground there to the hated Italians, the government in Athens had stubbornly refused to withdraw any part of the First Army in order to meet the German threat. Now the Greek troops in Albania were at risk of being cut off by an armored thrust, just as their fellow soldiers at the Metaxas Line had been.

Only units of the newly formed Allied Group W, consisting of the British and Commonwealth forces plus two inexperienced Greek divisions, stood

in the way of Stumme's panzers. In light of the capture of Salonika, the commander of the group, General Maitland Wilson, decided that a defense of Greece's northwestern frontier was futile. Instead, he would set up his main defensive line in an arc extending westward from the Aegean coast near Mount Olympus to the Aliakmon River—a position that conceded northern Greece to the Germans but guarded the main approaches to Athens. To delay the German onslaught, Wilson deployed a rear guard on the panzers' route of advance, ninety miles southwest of the Metaxas Line, and supported it with squadrons of the British Royal Air Force based south of his main line of defense. The mission of the task force was to hold its position "as long as possible—in any case, for three days."

Leading the German advance through the Monastir Gap on April 10 was a motorized infantry unit dear to the Führer: the Leibstandarte SS Adolf Hitler. As the men of the brigade rode across the frontier that morning, they found the going surprisingly easy. Lulled into a false sense of security, one company parked in the Greek border village of Niki, camouflaged their vehicles, and stripped down for a much-needed bath in a stream that ran through the town. "In the middle of the splashing and soap bubbles," one of the soldiers recalled, "we saw Bristol bombers heading toward us in three waves from the south." Unbeknown to the bathers, German antiaircraft batteries had already been set up near the town, and the flak guns were soon taking their toll. "Two bombers from the first formation were shot down," the SS man wrote, "and a third peeled off with clouds of smoke behind as it headed home."

The dripping infantrymen hurried into action without pausing to dress. "We loaded into the vehicles with weapons and ammunition and headed out," the soldier continued. "Uniforms and camouflage were donned on the way, and the chaos was brought into order. We moved forward in spurts. Once it was an attack from Spitfires that stopped us; another time, a demolished bridge blocked the way. It was already twilight as we raced through the next village, which lay under enemy artillery fire."

Early the next morning, April 11, the SS vanguard pushed through the town of Vevi and encountered a formidable obstacle—the bulk of the Allied rear guard, holding a narrow gap flanked by 3,000-foot-high ridges. Probing assaults by the Leibstandarte did little to shake the defenders that day. By the following morning, however, German tanks of the 9th Panzer Division had arrived on the scene. In a powerful assault that afternoon, the 33d Panzer Regiment pierced the Allied line. As the defenders withdrew, they could take some solace from the time that they had bought for General Wilson as he pieced together his main line to the south. But the delaying action had failed to help the Greek First Army, which was now trapped in

A Test of German Mobility in Greece

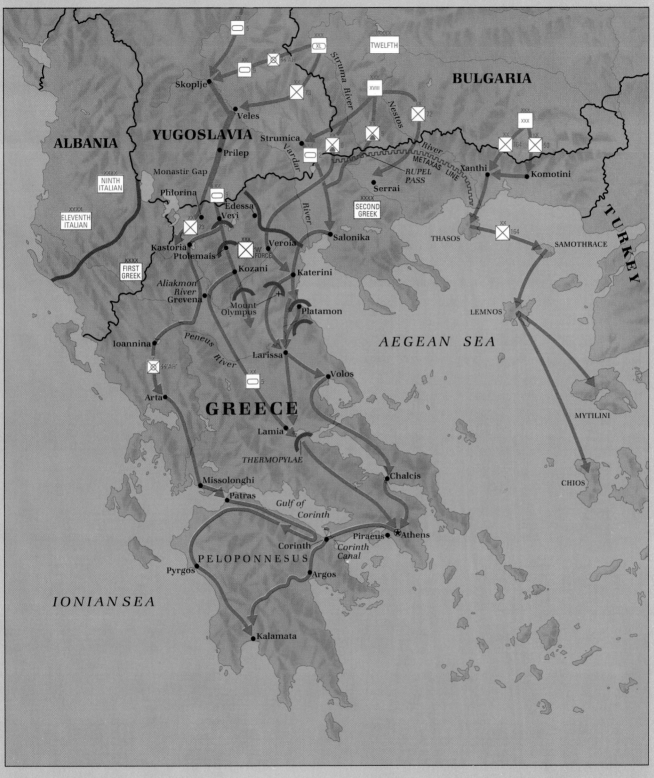

The invasion of Greece on April 6 proved German mobility over difficult terrain. While mountain troops headed south from Bulgaria to the Metaxas Line (*blue*), armored columns swung west through Yugoslavia and into Greece. The 2d Panzer Division reached Salonika on April 9. The XL Panzer Corps entered the Monastir Gap the next day. Over the next two weeks, German tanks advanced through the center of the country and along the east coast and met north of Thermopylae to drive on Athens. A smaller contingent veered west to cut off the Greek army in Albania, then turned south to occupy the Peloponnesus as task forces secured the islands.

Albania. Not until April 13 did the first Greek units begin to withdraw from Albania, and by then it was too late. That same day, General Stumme ordered the Leibstandarte, followed by the 73d Infantry Division, to head west toward the crossroads at Kastoria to cut off the Greek retreat. Within forty-eight hours, the Germans had captured Kastoria, blocking the First Army's most direct line of withdrawal, and were advancing toward the Adriatic to close the alternate escape routes. In the end, the Greek army had no choice except surrender.

While part of Stumme's corps headed for the Albanian border, the remainder followed the 9th Panzer Division along the road to Athens. To cope with the armored juggernaut descending on his main line, Wilson had only one British tank brigade, which was deployed south of Ptolemais, behind a barrier designed to stop the oncoming panzers in their tracks. British engineers had fashioned a natural tank trap by blowing up a bridge that carried the road over a six-foot-wide gully. The ditch was three feet deep and filled with water. Any tank wallowing into it would become a sitting duck for the British guns positioned on the surrounding hillsides.

When the 33d Panzer Regiment reached the trap shortly after noon on April 13, its commander recognized at once that any attempt to cross it would be suicidal. Only one route skirted the obstacle, and it led through a swamp that would normally have been considered unsuitable for tank traffic. The panzer leaders decided to gamble. The German tanks swung out across the swamp, moving at a snail's pace under intermittent artillery fire. Several of the vehicles bogged down, but most wallowed through the muck to dry ground, where thick brush and the rolling terrain cloaked them from enemy view. At dusk, they emerged with guns blazing on the flank of the British armored brigade. The British tanks turned about to meet the challenge but stood little chance. German warplanes had appeared on the horizon and were soon adding strafing and precision bombing from above to the panzers' fire below. By nightfall, the defenders were once again in retreat, leaving behind thirty-two shattered tanks. It was the first and last armored clash of the campaign.

As the battle raged at Ptolemais, General Wilson reluctantly reached a conclusion. Although his main line from Mount Olympus to the Aliakmon River was now fairly well established, he could scarcely expect it to hold out for long against a German invasion force that was far larger and had demonstrated an uncanny ability to circumvent any obstacle in its path. The progress of General Stumme's XL Panzer Corps was alarming enough, but in recent days General Böhme's XVIII Mountain Corps had regrouped in Salonika and was advancing down the Aegean coast. If either pincer broke through Wilson's line, the entire British Expeditionary Force would

Advancing toward Kastoria to block the Greek retreat from Albania, a mortar crew of the Leibstandarte SS Adolf Hitler hurries into position with gun tubes (*left*), a bipod to prop up the weapon (*center*), and boxes of shells (*right*). The SS unit captured the northern Greek city on April 15, taking 12,000 prisoners.

face a debacle reminiscent of Dunkirk. Wilson could expect no reinforcements from elsewhere in the Mediterranean. Indeed, the Greek commander in chief, General Alexander Papagos, was so certain of defeat that he now advocated a British evacuation in order to spare his nation further devastation. Under the circumstances, Wilson felt compelled to oblige him and attempt an orderly retreat. The Aliakmon line would be held by rearguard units in sufficient strength to permit the bulk of Wilson's group to retreat to the pass at Thermopylae—the storied gateway to Athens. Thermopylae would then become the last line of defense as the ill-fated expeditionary force embarked for Crete or Alexandria.

Wilson's plan worked well enough against Stumme's corps in central

Greece. On April 14, after refueling and replenishing ammunition stocks, Stumme's 9th Panzer rolled through the town of Kozani and forged a bridgehead across the Aliakmon. Then New Zealanders holding yet another narrow pass just beyond the river stopped the division cold. The tank traps and artillery batteries there were formidable, and Stumme had to resort to a time-consuming envelopment of the position. While part of his corps kept the New Zealanders busy, he sent the 5th Panzer Division—which had recently arrived from Yugoslavia after being detached from Kleist's panzer group—on a long detour to the west through Grevena and across the headwaters of the Aliakmon, beyond the fringe of the main British line. The roads were in dismal shape; it took the division four days to reach Grevena—long enough for Wilson to pull his western flank back toward Thermopylae in orderly fashion.

To the east, meanwhile, the situation was proving more perilous for the defenders. By April 14, Böhme's 2d Panzer Division had progressed down the Aegean coast to Katerini, and the mountain troops were following close behind. Ahead lay the town of Platamon, where the steep coastal range, crowned by Mount Olympus, dropped abruptly to the Aegean, leaving German armor little room to maneuver. There, on a ridge abutting the ruins of a seaside castle, a lone New Zealand battalion supported by a four-gun battery was charged with holding Wilson's right flank. The battalion's commander was told to expect infantry attacks only, since the terrain was ill suited for motorized units. But as daylight dwindled, the New Zealanders looking north from their ridgetop positions saw an ominous sight—a German motorcycle battalion was speeding down the coast. The tanks of the 3d Panzer Regiment, the division's vanguard, followed. They churned up the base of the ridge that evening and tested the Allied line. Once again, German armor was defying expectations.

The eventual breakthrough did not come easily. On April 15, Böhme's panzers made little headway in frontal assaults on the determined New Zealanders. In the meantime, a battalion of the 304th Rifle Regiment managed to thread up the ridge to the west and circle around the defenders' left. During the following morning, German troops and tanks descended like an avalanche on the enemy's flank and front, pressing the New Zealanders toward the sea. Soon the beleaguered battalion was retreating southward toward the Peneus Gorge, a gap in the coastal range leading inland to the Plain of Thessaly. Together, the narrow walls of the gorge and the river that ran through it posed the last significant natural obstacle to the invaders short of Thermopylae.

At the gorge, two Australian battalions and some artillery pieces reinforced the New Zealanders. But the German attack force grew in strength

Two tanks of the 2d Panzer Division—one of them belching smoke—lie abandoned in a ravine during the drive against the rear guard of the British Expeditionary Force at Platamon. A New Zealander later paid tribute to the panzers: "Seldom in war were tanks forced through such difficult terrain."

even faster, as the trailing elements of Böhme's corps poured down from Salonika. Böhme, his battered 5th Mountain Division still closing up from the rear, dispatched the 6th Mountain Division on an arduous trek over the coastal range and around the north ridge of the Peneus Gorge to its western exit, a flanking move timed to coincide with the 2d Panzer Division's direct assault through the gorge. For the men of the 6th Mountain, who had braved ice and snow to breach the Metaxas Line, the journey meant fresh hardships. As the troops climbed higher into the mountains on April 16, one sergeant recalled, "the trail grew worse and worse. It soon became dark. We had to inch our way forward. Suddenly, there was a heavy downpour such as I have never experienced in my life. Even under cover of our shelter halves, we were drenched within minutes. Small torrents came rushing down on the left. The mud was knee deep." Finally, one of the men fired his flare gun, lighting up their elusive objective for the night—a small village less than a quarter mile away. Shouting for joy, the troops slogged to shelter.

Better weather the next day enabled the panzers to probe the entrance to the canyon. Night fell before a full-scale battle could develop, but the stage was set for a showdown. At sunrise on April 18, the thunder of artillery and the clatter of machine guns drowned out the roar of the turbid river through the rocky gorge. A rude reception awaited the oncoming panzers: Both the road along the south bank and the rail line on the north bank were obstructed, and artillery batteries were well placed to exploit the inevitable traffic jams that resulted. The German tank commanders were challenged at every turn. At one spot, where there was no heavy artillery to confront the panzers, a group of fifteen or twenty Allied infantrymen surrounded a German tank and peppered it with rifle and light machine-gun fire. Undeterred, the behemoth creaked ahead, crushing two men beneath its tracks. Elsewhere, British artillery blasted the German armor at close range, leaving scorched hulks that trailing tanks had to push out of the way before the column could resume its harrowing crawl through the gauntlet.

If the Allied defenders had been confronted only with the 2d Panzer Division's direct assault up the gorge, they might have prolonged the struggle. But they were being pressed simultaneously at their flank and rear by Böhme's mountain troops, and by noon the pressure was beginning to tell. Through the morning, troops of the 6th Mountain Division had crept

Following the battle at Platamon, which was waged near the ruins of an old castle (*background*), panzers proceed warily along railroad tracks toward the Peneus Gorge. There, a blocked tunnel forced the tank crews to leave the tracks and ford the treacherous Peneus River.

down, under heavy artillery fire, to the north riverbank at the gorge's western exit. Determined to prevent a crossing that would trap the men deployed against the panzers in the gorge, the Allied forces were dug in on the far bank around the village of Evangelismos.

A German radio signalman described the advance of his battalion across the muddy torrent that afternoon. "The first of the infantrymen jumped down from the high bank and began wading into the raging waters," he wrote. "Soon a long chain of infantrymen could be seen across the river. Every man held onto the belt of the man in front of him. The enemy started firing with everything he had."

Following close behind the foot soldiers, the signalman had a particularly unenviable task: He and the other members of his detachment had to lug their heavy radio equipment across the river in order to keep the battalion's vanguard in contact with regimental headquarters. Their first

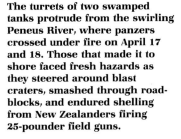

The turrets of two swamped tanks protrude from the swirling Peneus River, where panzers crossed under fire on April 17 and 18. Those that made it to shore faced fresh hazards as they steered around blast craters, smashed through roadblocks, and endured shelling from New Zealanders firing 25-pounder field guns.

sensation on entering the river with their burden was one of relief—they were sweating profusely in the heat, and the flowing cold water was bracing. But it was small comfort under the circumstances. "We had to fight against the current so as not to be swept downstream," the signalman recalled. "Cones of machine-gun fire splashed into the water in front of us, then to our right and behind us."

Straining toward shore, they collapsed on the sandy bank with their precious equipment until they could summon the strength to make a dash for cover in the trees that lined the road. Once in the trees, they could see that the troops who had preceded them were preparing to storm the enemy strongholds in the town. Then the signalmen witnessed a crucial development: Several tanks rumbled out of the gorge to join the battle. Despite all the obstacles in their path, the panzers had broken through— welcome news that the radio detachment soon broadcast. "We quickly set up our radio station," the signalman wrote, "and I proudly transmitted the battalion commander's message to regiment headquarters: 'Battalion has crossed river after heavy fighting and reached road to Larissa. Our own tanks already advancing.'"

With the road sealed behind them, the defenders in the gorge had no hope of prevailing. Yet few realized their plight at once; they were fighting in isolated units and lacked radio equipment. In any case, their mission was to defend the position at all cost. Many of them held out until nightfall, exacting a price but paying even more dearly. The 21st New Zealand Battalion was virtually annihilated.

Meanwhile, beyond the gorge, Germans were hurrying southwestward to intercept the main Allied force. The two days it had taken Böhme's corps to break through from Platamon had been just enough for Wilson to draw back his right wing and prevent an envelopment. But the Germans were nipping at the heels of his men, leaving them no time to destroy vital supplies. When the lead elements of Böhme's corps reached Larissa early on April 19, they found ample stocks of fuel and food that would serve them well in the days ahead.

Over the next few days, the two armored pincers of the invasion force converged on Thermopylae. Böhme's corps reached the port city of Volos on April 21, then hurried to Lamia, northwest of Thermopylae. Meanwhile, the 5th Panzer Division—dispatched by Stumme a week earlier on the wide flanking movement through Grevena—was streaming into Lamia from the northwest. By April 23, German reconnaissance units were probing Wilson's lines at Thermopylae, where in ancient times a few hundred Spartan and allied warriors had held off a vastly superior Persian army long enough to ensure the safe withdrawal of the main Greek force. The memory

Advance elements of the XL Panzer Corps, moving through central Greece under the command of General Georg Stumme (*at left in inset*), construct a pontoon bridge over the Peneus River west of Larissa.

of that stand inspired the British prime minister, for one, to hope for similar heroics now. "The intervening ages fell away," Churchill wrote later. "Why not one more undying feat of arms?"

In fact, Wilson's rear guard was defending a position that bore little resemblance to the narrow coastal strip the ancient Spartans had once held. Over the centuries, alluvial deposits had extended the coast, widening the gateway for invaders along the sea. And to complicate matters, the defenders had to cover not one route but two, because the road south split at Thermopylae. One branch continued along the coast, the other wound upward into the hills. Thus the meager rearguard detachment had to be divided. The 6th New Zealand Brigade stood vigil on the coast, and the 19th Australian Brigade blocked the road in the hills near Skamnos, several miles from the sea.

The German offensive at Thermopylae followed the now-familiar pattern of simultaneous frontal and flanking assaults. Once again, the task of enveloping the enemy fell to the 6th Mountain Division. Its lead battalions reached Lamia on April 23, passed straight through, and began an all-night climb into the hills on a footpath that circled west of the route defended by the Australians. The German troops paused around dawn to rest their exhausted pack animals and continued to wait as Stukas dive-bombed the Australian position. The mountain infantrymen advanced on the enemy's left flank around nine o'clock and soon discovered that the Stuka attack had failed to eliminate the defenses. The Australians loosed a hail of fire from well-concealed machine-gun nests. The Germans fought forward through rocky ravines that offered effective cover but impeded their progress. It was afternoon before the first German units flushed the defenders from their gun emplacements and penetrated the Allied line. The Australians tried gamely to stem the breach, but shellfire from mountain artillery, brought into position by the pack animals, foiled their counterattacks. Around six that evening, the defenders finally abandoned their crumbling stronghold and retreated southward.

Other German mountain units had meanwhile advanced on the New Zealanders' location athwart the coast road. By late afternoon, the alpine troops were pressing the New Zealanders along their western flank, while a mixed force, including heavy armor, was attempting to punch through the New Zealand brigade head-on. It was a tight spot for the German tanks, which had to advance through a narrow corridor of marshland that allowed little room to maneuver and, in many places, proved too soft to support large vehicles. Slowed by the terrain or bogged down entirely, the panzers proved easy prey for the enemy batteries. By nightfall, more than a dozen German tanks had been knocked out.

After breaking through the final British cordon at Thermopylae on April 24, German troops trudge toward Athens as staff cars drive past. Rough roads had exhausted the German army's supply of spare tires, knocking out more than a third of the vehicles and slowing the last phase of the campaign.

Despite such successes, the defenders had no illusions about holding out for long. In the midst of the fighting that afternoon, the New Zealand commander, Major General Sir Bernard Freyberg, received personal orders to report to an embarkation point—a clear sign that his superiors regarded his position as untenable. Freyberg replied coolly that he was busy "fighting a battle" and remained at his post. But German pressure continued into the night, threatening to collapse his isolated position at any time. Around midnight, the New Zealanders began to withdraw.

As the Germans poured through at Thermopylae, the British stepped up the pace of their evacuation efforts. The logical point of embarkation would have been the major port of Piraeus, near Athens, but the capacity of that

harbor had been greatly reduced on the first night of the campaign, when German bombers taking off from Sicily blew up a British ship loaded with 250 tons of dynamite, setting off a chain of explosions that rocked the pilots in their cockpits and shattered windows up to ten miles away. As a result of the damage, the British had to rely on a number of additional ports, including several on the Peloponnesus, the country's prominent southern peninsula, which was separated from the mainland by a canal cutting across the Isthmus of Corinth.

The German high command made a bold attempt to leapfrog ahead of the fleeing Allied troops and sever their route of retreat across the isthmus. On April 26, two battalions of German paratroopers floated down over the canal and seized the bridge. As it turned out, this airborne coup accomplished little, since most of the Allied troops bound for the Peloponnesus had already crossed the span. Yet several thousand Allied soldiers who escaped the snare at Corinth were taken prisoner in the next few days, when they failed to reach their assigned harbors before the last of the rescue ships departed.

Meanwhile, the victorious German forces descended on Athens. Motorcyclists of the 2d Panzer Division entered the Greek capital on April 27 and raised the swastika over the Acropolis to mark their triumph. For Hitler, who had followed the course of the campaign from his special train near the Reich-Yugoslavian frontier, the fall of the ancient city was gratifying but less than decisive. His army had conquered Greece in just three weeks at a cost of roughly 5,000 casualties, including 1,100 dead. By contrast, the

In a daring effort to intercept British troops retreating to the Peloponnesus across the Corinth Canal *(left)*, German paratroopers descended at dawn on April 26 and seized the bridge *(center)*. Minutes later, as the sun rose over the canal, a British shell touched off demolition charges *(right)*, destroying the structure and killing a number of paratroopers. By evening, however, the Germans had strung a new bridge over the gap and were bringing troops across in order to continue the pursuit. The photographer who snapped the picture at center was one of those killed in the explosion.

British had lost a quarter of their 52,000-man expeditionary force, including 11,000 captured. Some 2,100 had been killed or wounded—the majority of them victims of Luftwaffe air raids, which sank twenty-six troop-laden ships during the evacuation.

Still, nearly 40,000 soldiers had escaped, most of them sailing to the one significant parcel of Greek territory that remained unvanquished. Since April 6, German and Italian ships had been plying the waters off Greece with relative impunity, securing one island after another for the Axis—with the notable exception of distant Crete. Now tens of thousands of retreating Allied troops were taking refuge on the island, much to the Führer's dismay. So long as the Allies held Crete, Adolf Hitler's Balkan campaign would remain unfinished. Allied naval or air strikes launched from the island would jeopardize any German operations in the Mediterranean or southern Europe. Crete must be captured, the German high command realized, and it made plans accordingly.

British intelligence soon learned of the German intentions through intercepted and decoded messages. On April 28, Prime Minister Churchill neatly forecast the bloody turn that the campaign was about to take in a communiqué to General Sir Archibald Wavell, commander in chief of British forces in the Middle East. "It seems clear from our information that a heavy airborne attack by German troops and bombers will soon be made on Crete," Churchill wrote. "Let me know what forces you have on the island and what your plans are. It ought to be a fine opportunity for killing the parachute troops. The island must be stubbornly defended." ✚

Favored with fine weather, dive bombers return from a sortie against the Metaxas Line *(map, inset)* on April 6, 1941. German troops watched gratefully as the Stukas approached the Greek works in the early light. "My God," a soldier uttered, "it looks like there's no end of them!"

Assault on a Mountain Stronghold

The German mountain troops assigned to storm the Greek border in early April 1941 faced a towering challenge. After marching more than 250 miles from Rumania to southern Bulgaria, they had to ascend the steep, snow-clad slopes of the Belasica Range *(left)*, then smash through the Metaxas Line—one of the most imposing fortified barriers in the world. Laid out in the 1930s by the Greek premier, Ioannis Metaxas, as a bulwark against rival Bulgaria, the cordon made the most of the region's natural strong points: On peaks along the frontier ridge, engineers had fashioned cavernous fortresses, each consisting of several bunkers that were connected by tunnels. One of the sturdiest of these works stood atop Istibei Mountain—the linchpin in a complex of ten high bastions guarding the vital Struma River pass. At Istibei alone, a well-stocked garrison of 500 soldiers stood ready in a network of twenty-five bunkers bristling with more than forty machine guns and several artillery pieces. The bunkers' occupants were linked to a command center by telephone and speaking tubes and could retreat, if necessary, into a labyrinth of corridors that would take the uninitiated hours to negotiate.

The Germans set out to soften up Istibei and its neighboring strongholds by pounding the bunkers from the air. But the Stuka pilots who swooped down at dawn on April 6 found it difficult to distinguish the artfully camouflaged Greek works from the surrounding terrain, and their bombs did little more than rearrange the landscape. Heartened nonetheless by the dramatic aerial display and supporting artillery fire, troops of the 5th Mountain Division advanced gingerly up the slopes with their cumbersome gear, encountering little resistance at first. One of the men attacking Istibei described the scene: "The dark file climbs higher and higher. The men are moving up in an erect position. Apparently, the enemy has not yet recovered from the shock." In fact, the resilient Greeks were preparing a nasty surprise for the Germans, few of whom would maintain an erect posture for long.

An artilleryman *(foreground)* sets the fuse of a shell for a 150-mm howitzer aimed at Greek positions on the distant ridge. Shock troops *(inset)* brace to move out under cover of the barrage.

Even before the Stukas and the heavy artillery in the foothills completed their opening bombardment of the Metaxas Line, shock troops of the 5th Mountain Division began their assault on the heavily bunkered ridge. These were precarious moments for the men of the foremost units, who advanced immediately behind the falling bombs and shells. Then the end of the barrage brought fresh concern, because it immediately became apparent that few of the targets had been seriously damaged. The embrasures on most of the bunkers were open for business, and the Greek guns were spitting fire.

While the shock troops probed for weak spots in the enemy line, mountain artillery units hauled their light guns forward in order to try to neutralize the Greeks at short range. It was no task for the delicate. As one crew of five strained at ropes to drag their piece up an incline, a sixth man trailed behind with two forty-five-pound boxes of shells. Sweating and puffing, the carrier set down his load to catch his breath. "Don't knock yourself out, buddy," one of his seasoned mates gibed. "In my day, we ran races with boxes like those."

The crew commander put a stop to the banter and directed the gunners' attention to a suspicious pile of branches. A well-aimed shot scattered the camouflage and revealed two dark gun barrels poking through embrasures. Having laid the target bare, the German artillerists rammed shell after shell into the breech and blasted away. The shots failed to crack the concrete walls of the bunker, but for a while they kept silent the guns housed there—and any pause in the Greek firestorm enabled German infantry-

78

men to expediently swarm forward.

To reach the bunkers, the foot soldiers had to complete a hazardous course. The slopes below the embrasures had been cleared of trees and planted with booby traps and thickets of barbed wire. Trenches projecting from the sides of the bunkers formed a second barrier, although the Greeks were stretched too thin to occupy all the trenches in force. The most daunting feature of the defense works was the clever alignment of the bunkers themselves, which enabled the defenders in one enclosure to cover the exposed flank of a neighboring position.

Fire from the bunkers was so intense at some points that the advancing mountain troops were stopped in their tracks and had to hunker down in the freshly blasted shell craters that pocked the landscape. On the steep slopes of Rupesco Mountain, whose snow-shrouded bunkers had remained unscathed in the opening barrage, the Germans abandoned any hope of attacking and assumed a defensive posture. Elsewhere, soldiers crawled up the incline on their bellies and arduously sheared a trail through the barbed fields with wire cutters—an effort in which more than a few men were torn apart by exploding mines.

Once a path had been cleared to a trench, the Germans used it to their advantage. Tossing hand grenades to scatter the Greek riflemen, mountain troops poured into the trench. They were then in position to come at a bunker laterally while avoiding the covering fire from its neighbor. To reach their goal, they had to pick their way over bodies and subdue any surviving riflemen in the narrow ditch, all the time

Their packs bulging, members of a German flanking patrol seek the path of least resistance along a rugged, snow-covered slope.

Carrying a gas-mask canister on his back, a mountaineer digs in with his cleats to scale a cliff.

Germans crawl along a captured trench near an abandoned guard post to reach a Greek bunker.

taking care not to poke their heads above the lip. As one attacker recalled, "The bullets started flying immediately if a German helmet as much as became visible over the top of the trench."

In the crucial battle for Istibei Mountain, the Germans combined such frontal assaults with deft flanking moves. For all its strengths, the Metaxas Line was not an unbroken wall. The frontier ridge was laced with numerous defiles, and the Greeks lacked the troops to guard every passage. Through the morning hours, mountain-wise German soldiers—equipped with sturdy boots whose spiked soles clawed at the treacherous terrain—found ways around the heavily fortified approaches. Some of the men had spent youthful years clambering up rocky slopes in Bavaria and Austria, and the paths they negotiated here were no more difficult. What made the task so exacting was the heavy gear they carried—a punishing load that included hand grenades, a rifle and ammunition, a shelter half for sleeping, several days' rations, entrenching tools, flare guns, and a gas-mask canister (a precaution that proved unnecessary). Making good time despite the burden, the flanking troops were soon descending on the Istibei bunkers from above even as the main units came storming up the slope to seize the trenches.

With the enemy in sight, the mountain troops were in position to bring their full arsenal to bear. Machine guns light enough to be carried by a single soldier enabled individual Germans to trade fire with the Greeks on an equal footing. Meanwhile, engineers prepared satchel charges—compact bundles of explosives with handles—for

Glimpses of the fighting for the bunkers reveal the array of weapons that the Germans committed to the assault, including flamethrowers *(left)* fed from a heavy tank strapped onto the operator's back; MG 34 machine guns *(below)*, which fired fifteen rounds per second; and satchel charges *(bottom right)*, handy bombs that could be wedged into the bunkers' embrasures.

special delivery. A favorite tactic of those approaching a bunker from above was to creep onto the ledge above the embrasure, wait for a pause in the spate of bullets from the Greek guns, then lean over and stuff the satchel into the opening. Yet alert defenders could thwart the bold tactic by pushing the satchel out before it exploded.

Germans creeping through the trenches planted their explosives at the armored doors that linked the excavations to the bunkers and connecting tunnels. One witness saw four combat engineers wedge their satchels together against one heavy portal. "They hugged the ground just five meters away," he wrote, "with their steel helmets providing the only protection against the expected blast. But everything worked out. Following the detonation of the charge and the rain of dirt and debris, they threw a smoke grenade into the smoldering entranceway and another powerful charge. Inside, there was not a sound to be heard."

Where situations prohibited close work of this type, the Germans targeted the embrasures with flamethrowers, which could shoot a searing jet up to eighty feet. The weapons took their toll, but they could not ensure the surrender of the survivors in the bunkers, who could withdraw to another portion of the works and return later with reinforcements unless the casemates were reduced to rubble. Despite the sophisticated tools at their disposal, the mountain troops found that one of the most efficient ways to neutralize a bunker was simply to shovel rocks and dirt between the embrasures and the wire camouflage netting in front of them. One attacker noted with satisfac-

A German *(above)* guards the shattered entryway to a tunnel linking the Greek positions.

A captured bunker *(right)* bears the scars of the German assault, which tore holes in the protective wire mesh used to hang camouflage, exposed the steel grillwork that reinforced the concrete structure, and clogged the embrasures with debris.

tion that the Greeks could not push out the obstructing debris, which became firmly wedged in the mesh. "That's the way to get at them!" the German exclaimed.

Profiting by such devices, the mountain troops were near victory at Istibei by early afternoon when the besieged Greeks turned the tables, calling in artillery fire and, with bayonets fixed, launching reckless counterattacks from their shelters. "Now we were holding the mountain," one German recalled later, "and they were trying to storm it." Time after time, machine-gun fire cut down the Greeks as they charged their enemies, who were ensconced in trenches, craters, and shattered bunkers.

By nightfall, the pressure on the mountain troops was easing, and reinforcements came up to relieve the hardest-hit units. Through the night, tireless engineers groped toward the remaining bunkers by the eerie light of flares and shellbursts to seal up embrasures or plant fresh charges. As a gray dawn broke over the mountain, German troops shivering in the rain and sleet thrilled to a crescendo of explosions that sent large chunks of jagged concrete and steel flying through the air. The crowning blast came from the armored cupola at the top of the mountain, which had served the Greeks as an observation and command post. With this defensive keystone obliterated and few of the surrounding bunkers left intact, the fortress at Istibei was doomed.

German mountain troops began to penetrate the mazelike tunnels in an effort to root out surviving opponents, but the pursuit was slow and treacherous. At a quarter past eleven, the Greek commandant reluctantly conceded defeat and

A battle flag flying from the heights heralds the victory that gave the Germans control of the Struma River valley *(background)*.

Disconsolate Greek prisoners await transport. They were later released when Greece fell.

Amid signs of spring, mountain troops file past an abandoned Greek staff car as they head south to continue the campaign.

emerged with his garrison. Few defenders had been killed, but many were wounded; their bowed heads and blighted expressions told of their fruitless ordeal. For the Germans, who had dreaded the prospect of another murderous day on the slopes, the surrender was a stunning vindication of their efforts. As one soldier put it, "A wonderful sense of superiority came over us, an indescribably unique and powerful feeling of victory."

At other fortresses nearby, however, the fighting was not over. On Popotlivitsa Mountain, defiant Greeks left their bunkers and stormed the enemy lines so ferociously they knocked some of the Germans from their feet and, tumbling down the hillside, grappled with the intruders until one soldier's stranglehold or knife thrust finished off the other. On remote Rupesco Mountain, the Germans remained pinned down for a second day, suffering from exposure. When the Greeks there finally abandoned the works late on April 9, the mountain troops entered to find dead defenders frozen where they had fallen, their faces shrouded with a thin sheet of ice.

Such heroic stands by isolated Greek bastions along the Metaxas Line did not alter the outcome of the battle, which was decided when the Germans broke through at Istibei on April 7. By that afternoon, German troops were pouring down the southern slope of the frontier range to claim the Struma River valley and its routes to the Aegean. As the soldiers descended, they left winter behind and entered a budding landscape tinted with lilacs and almond blossoms—tantalizing emblems of a gentle spring in a long season of war.

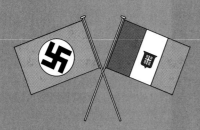

Farcical Fall of a Proud Army

The surrender of Greece's First Army smacked more of comic opera than Greek tragedy. The bizarre episode began on April 15, 1941, when advance units of the Leibstandarte SS Adolf Hitler, a motorized brigade leading the German thrust through the mountains of northwestern Greece, drove into the key town of Kastoria. The German presence threatened the rear of Greek forces fighting the Italians in nearby Albania and also sealed off roads and mountain passes the Greeks might have used to retreat southward.

Realizing that his army was in a tight spot, the Greek commander, General George Tsolakoglu, decided to negotiate. He sent emissaries to find the Leibstandarte's General Josef "Sepp" Dietrich. Tsolakoglu's dual motives were to save pointless bloodshed and to deal with the victorious Germans rather than suffer the indignity, as he saw it, of surrendering to Italian forces that he had driven back into Albania.

Dietrich, an early Nazi sidekick of Hitler himself, was astonished to be offered the surrender of an entire army. He quickly accepted the Greek tender. But almost at once, the amicable arrangement began to fall apart. On hearing of the surrender, the Italian dictator, Benito Mussolini, flew into a rage, insisting to Hitler that his forces be part of the pact—precisely what Tsolakoglu wanted to avoid. Unwilling to risk the German-Italian alliance simply to assuage Greek pride, Hitler disowned the agreements reached by his frontline officers, ensuring a farce of several acts before a final surrender could be achieved (*following pages*).

Advancing through what one soldier called a "heavenly landscape,"

motorized artillery of the Leibstandarte SS Adolf Hitler passes Lake Kastoria as it drives southward through the Greek mountains.

Greek soldiers, one in the dashing uniform of the select Evzone mountain infantry, display white flags as they await the Germans.

Backed by his staff, the Leibstandarte's Sepp Dietrich *(center)* greets General Tsolakoglu *(foreground, left)* and his chief aide.

An Amicable Offer to Capitulate

The first encounter between Germans and Greeks went off with barely a hitch. The Leibstandarte was deploying to attack a vital pass, one soldier recalled, when "the enemy suddenly stopped firing" and several Greek officers with white flags emerged from their positions and asked to be taken to the commander of the German force.

Reacting quickly, the SS troops radioed their headquarters to summon Sepp Dietrich, who hurried forward. By early evening, he and General Tsolakoglu were closeted in the Greek commander's headquarters, amiably discussing surrender terms. The only problem, an SS officer remembered, was that the Germans could not read the pact, which had been typed in Greek. By the time it had been translated and retyped in German, the two generals had left together to announce the surrender to their men. The typists overtook them, however, and, sitting next to each other under the black pines of the pass, Tsolakoglu and Dietrich signed the documents by flashlight.

Surrendering Again – and Again

The surrender seemed settled, but by the next morning, the bilingual pact was fast coming unglued. The difficulties began when General Dietrich's tradition-minded superior, Field Marshal Wilhelm List, condemned the document as casual and incomplete. Tsolakoglu found himself signing a second document, this time with List, that specified the terms of surrender and included a provision allowing Greek officers to keep their side arms.

Mussolini, furious now at being excluded from *two* surrenders, fired off irate messages to Hitler. The duce also refused to abide by the cease-fire and urged his troops in Albania to advance against Tsolakoglu's half-disbanded army.

Fearful for his men, the Greek general had little choice but to accept another arrangement. Dietrich's SS men kept the Italian army at bay while Tsolakoglu, General Alfred Jodl—a representative sent by Hitler himself—and Italian officers negotiated a third surrender.

Their war over, Greek soldiers smile and wave at a passing German vehicle as they trudge toward an assembly point for prisoners of war.

In Salonika on April 23, 1941, Generals Tsolakoglu (seated, far right) and Jodl (seated, second from left) craft a third version of the Greek surrender with an Italian general (back to camera).

German troops shielding the Greek First Army from attack by the Italians stop a pair of the duce's soldiers (foreground) at a bridge spanning the Saranta-poros River on the Albanian border. The river formed a line of demarcation between German and Italian forces.

Eyes right, parading Italian infantrymen in a truck pass Field Marshal Wilhelm List's reviewing position.

A Subdued Victory Parade

Not content to have involved Italy in the surrender of the Greek First Army, Mussolini vaingloriously demanded a victory parade through Athens once all of Greece had capitulated. The idea vexed the Germans, who were busy planning the next phase of the war; they saw nothing to be gained from rubbing sensitive Greek noses in defeat.

Once more, however, the Führer bowed to his Axis partner and approved the parade—provided that the celebration was restrained and the Italian share in it modest.

After the shooting stopped on April 30, portions of a single panzer division and some German mountain troops gathered in small towns between Athens and Corinth to bathe and smarten up. Then, accompanied by a regiment of Italian motorized infantry, the victors paraded through the streets of the storied Greek capital with a minimum of fanfare. Some Athenians turned out, and a few applauded as the Wehrmacht passed in review. Mussolini's legion, however, was met with absolute silence.

Marching within sight of the Acropolis *(background)*, **German mountain troops pass in close order through Athens's palace square.**

Winged Invasion of an Aegean Isle

A German paratrooper appropriates a donkey to carry an injured comrade to safety during the fighting for Crete in May 1941. On the first day of the battle, nearly half of the invasion force was killed, injured, or captured.

eneral Julius Ringel, commander of the Wehrmacht's 5th Mountain Division, considered himself a man of culture, and he was keenly aware of his historic surroundings on the morning of May 3, 1941. "The portico of the Parthenon in the blue Aegean summer sky beams down upon us from the Acropolis," he wrote contentedly. "The walls of the houses of this proud city, in a mixture of Paris and old-Athens architecture, glisten white and yellow in the dazzling sun."

The general was enjoying everything about this day in Athens. A pleasant breeze wafted across the plaza in front of the Greek royal palace. Not only did the draft relieve the heat, it provided a visual thrill as well. Outside the royal palace, the flagpole stood bare, but across the plaza the black, white, and red colors of the Third Reich fluttered splendidly in the wind.

Precisely at nine o'clock, a reviewing party headed by the commander of the Twelfth Army, Field Marshal Wilhelm List, ceremonially took its place. The sound of approaching bands and the tread of military boots filled the ancient square and swelled Ringel's heart. "Athens's soil," he wrote, "with its culture of many thousand years, now witnesses the victory parade of the German army."

When the celebration ended, Ringel started toward his car, looking forward to a tour of the city's antiquities. On his way, he encountered an old friend, Major General Wilhelm Süssmann, commander of the XI Air Corps's elite 7th Paratroop Division. The two congratulated each other on the victory in Greece and exchanged small talk until Süssmann smiled and said, "Let's hope for real good comradeship and collaboration during our next operation." Ringel gave him a blank look. "Haven't you heard?" asked Süssmann. The 5th Mountain Division was to join his paratroop and glider forces in Operation Mercury—the imminent invasion of Crete.

Stunned, Ringel rushed to his headquarters. There he found orders but no special instructions for an operation that would be very difficult, indeed, unprecedented. Aware that most of his men had never even seen the inside of an aircraft, Ringel set to work to prepare them for a flight of "hundreds of kilometers over the sea for the conquest of a rocky, hilly island."

The Bold Plan to Seize a Forbidding Coast

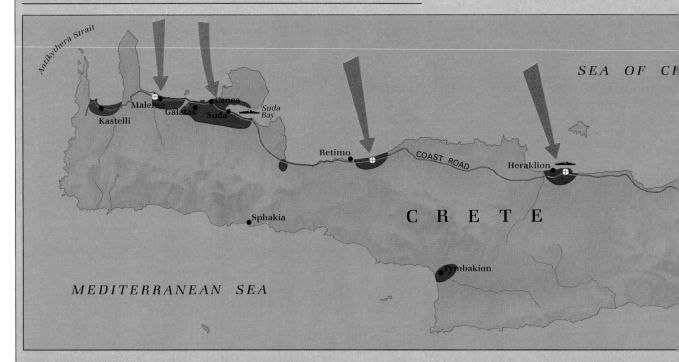

The plan to conquer Crete was both ambitious and risky. On the first day, shock troops landing by parachute and glider were to capture four key points along eighty miles of the island's northern coast. These targets, linked by Crete's only paved road, included the unfinished but usable runway near Maleme; the Allied command center outside Canea and the nearby Royal Navy facility on Suda Bay; another unfinished landing strip at Retimo; and the airfield and harbor at Heraklion. The assault would come in two waves: the drops at Maleme and Canea in the morning and those at Retimo and Heraklion in the afternoon. On the second day, reinforcements would be airlifted into the secure airfields and augmented by seaborne reinforcements.

Despite its isolation (60 miles from the Greek mainland, at the southern extremity of the Aegean Sea), its modest size (160 miles long by 35 miles at its widest), and its pastoral economy, Crete had long held the attention of world powers. Indeed, as the cradle of one of the earliest human civilizations, the Minoan, it had been a great power itself 1,500 years before the birth of Christ. After the sudden and mysterious demise of the Minoans, Crete had been a pawn in several imperial conflicts: between Byzantine and Arab, Ottoman and Venetian, Greek and Turk. Now in 1941 it was to become a battlefield in the struggle between the Axis and the Allied powers—and the site of a revolutionary experiment in warfare.

Fate had endowed Crete with enormous strategic importance in the fight to control southeastern Europe and the eastern Mediterranean. British forces on Crete, swelled in number by the troops evacuated from Greece, posed an intolerable threat to Hitler's southeastern flank, especially if the Allies were to use the island to launch bombing raids on the oil fields of Rumania, the source of much of the Wehrmacht's fuel. If, on the other hand, the Germans took the island, it would provide a base for the Luftwaffe to counter the Royal Navy in the eastern Mediterranean.

The German high command had contemplated an attack on Crete since the previous autumn. In November, Hitler had mentioned to Benito Mussolini the possibility of a "lightning occupation of Crete," but such talk was easy; daunting tactical problems confronted the military planners. Not only

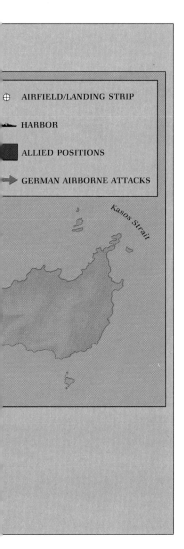

AIRFIELD/LANDING STRIP

HARBOR

ALLIED POSITIONS

GERMAN AIRBORNE ATTACKS

Kasos Strait

was Crete an island, it was protected by the Royal Navy and robustly garrisoned by ground forces. Obviously, the solution was to mount an airborne operation, making use of the Luftwaffe's almost-total control of the air. But there were numerous unknown factors and, therefore, huge risks.

In all previous airborne operations, panzer columns racing overland had swiftly relieved the paratroop and glider assault teams that led the attack. This time, except for a hastily assembled and highly vulnerable seaborne contingent, the invasion force would have to rely on the Luftwaffe for everything from reinforcements and ammunition to medical supplies, food, and even drinking water. This unequivocal dependence on aircraft simplified the selection of primary objectives on the island; the invaders would immediately have to seize and hold at least one airfield—or they faced certain annihilation.

For all its perils, the invasion plan's most ardent advocate was the officer who would have to carry it out—the founder of Germany's airborne arm, Lieut. General Kurt Student. Surprisingly quiet and austere for a leader of paratroopers, Student had been a combat pilot in World War I and had been wounded twice in dogfights over the Western Front. Hermann Göring had given him command of the Luftwaffe's new paratroop division in 1938. Student had honed his men to a razor edge for the invasions of 1940 and performed so remarkably—while suffering yet another wound—that he became a national celebrity. A few jealous colleagues sniffed that Student's success owed more to Hitler's favor than to ability, but the discerning knew him to be shrewd, cool, and possessed of a keen military intuition, qualities that would serve him well in the harrowing days ahead.

Student now commanded the Luftwaffe's XI Air Corps, which consisted of General Süssmann's 7th Paratroop, plus the 22d Luftlande, or Air-Landing, Division, specially trained to follow the paratroopers in Ju 52 transports. Student was convinced that his men could contribute to grand strategy and was anxious to dispel the notion that they were useful merely as saboteurs or commandos. He saw in the invasion of Crete an opportunity to prove his case to the Führer and the world. Student had no illusions about the dangers awaiting his men on Crete, but he knew that if any troops could pull off such a coup, it would be his "hunters from the sky."

Founded as an adjunct to massed panzers and Stukas in the German arsenal of blitzkrieg weapons, the paratroop units had swiftly demonstrated their effectiveness. In the spring campaign of 1940, they had opened the way for the invasion of Belgium and the Netherlands by seizing bridges over the Rhine-Maas estuary and capturing the massive fortress of Eben Emael. Using gliders, two officers and eighty-three men had landed directly atop

the fort and neutralized it for twenty-four hours, until advancing ground forces relieved them. Instead of boasting about these exploits, the Germans astutely employed reverse psychology and declared all details top secret.

The ploy worked brilliantly. Germany's enemies soon endowed the airborne troops with a great and baleful reputation. They were said to have dropped in hordes across the Lowlands and France, often disguised as French or British soldiers, sometimes garbed as priests, postmen, or marketwomen. On May 21, 1941, the Dutch foreign minister in exile told a press conference in London that parachutists dressed as nuns, monks, and streetcar conductors had overrun his country. And the British high command, a year after the campaign in France, still believed that the Germans had available at least six paratroop divisions. The ability of the paratrooper to bypass any natural obstacle or man-made defense and to appear suddenly in a vulnerable rear area bedeviled Allied commanders, who were already hard-pressed to block the unconventional thrusts of blitzkrieg. So far, however, the Allies had done little to gather information about the strength and tactics of German airborne troops or to develop countermeasures against them.

The Allies would have been surprised to learn that there had never been more than a single paratroop division in the Wehrmacht's order of battle. And Student's troops had never worn disguises, which were a trick beneath the exceptional soldiers who wore the badge with the plunging golden eagle. The men were mostly young—the average age in one battalion was little more than eighteen years—and all were volunteers who had exhibited the physical conditioning, judgment, independence, and raw courage required to jump from an airplane, form up under heavy fire, and attack an enemy that was usually better armed and numerically superior.

Most of the youthful warriors had spent their adolescence immersed in the vengeful tenets of Nazi ideology. They represented, as Churchill later wrote, "the flame of the Hitler Youth movement, an ardent embodiment of the Teutonic spirit of revenge for the defeat of 1918. The flower of German manhood was expressed in these valiant, highly trained, and completely devoted parachute troops." Hitler would pay the supreme compliment of calling them the "toughest fighters in the Wehrmacht, tougher even than the Waffen-SS." But on the whole, Student's paratroopers did not adopt the racist attitudes that made the SS units scorn their enemies and commit atrocities. It was enough to fervently believe in the unofficial commandment of the parachutist: "Be as nimble as a greyhound, as tough as leather, as hard as Krupp steel, and so you shall be the German warrior incarnate."

Despite the quality of its men, however, the paratroop division had to overcome severe disadvantages implicit in its operations. The large, lum-

A student practices descent maneuvers in a harness hung from the training hall's ceiling.

Training Hunters from the Sky

Every candidate for Germany's elite paratroop units was a carefully screened volunteer. Before a soldier could wear the coveted diving-eagle badge of the parachutist, however, he had to complete a gru-eling eight-week training course that included six practice jumps. According to Kurt Student, commander of the airborne troops, the program was designed to instill "a comradeship wider and deeper than in any other corps."

The first jump school opened in 1936 in the Saxon town of Stendal. Others followed in Wittstock, Mecklenburg, Braunschweig, and, later, Châteaudun in occupied France.

Trainees underwent exercises and drills that familiarized them with every aspect of jumping. Unlike Allied paratroopers, who jumped feet first, the Germans exited the aircraft in a forward horizontal leap. They learned to maneuver facing downwind as they neared the ground, enabling them to fall forward onto their hands and knees, somersault, and spring quickly to their feet.

Wearing parachutes with static lines to simulate actual conditions, trainees leap from a parked Ju 52. In a real jump, the chute opened automatically after the weight of the falling paratrooper tautened the static line attached to the transport.

Novice German paratroopers somersault over crouching comrades in a drill to improve their agility. Upon hitting the ground, the men performed a tuck and roll that softened the impact of landing and readily propelled them to their feet.

Working in pairs, trainees learn how to pack a parachute properly. Each paratrooper was responsible for his own chute—an item on which his life depended.

bering transport planes and the slowly descending parachutists were extremely vulnerable to concentrated fire from the ground. If the drops were made from higher altitudes in order to spare the aircraft, then the paratroopers would be exposed to fire longer and dispersed more widely. Troops dropped under cover of darkness or in widely scattered areas might be more likely to reach the ground unscathed, but it would take them so long to reassemble that they would lose the critical advantage of surprise. Eventually, Student and his planners decided that the sturdy trimotor Ju 52 transports could withstand groundfire better than individual soldiers, and that the benefits of concentrated drops outweighed the danger. It would become standard procedure for the Ju 52s—twelve men per plane— to approach at a maximum altitude of 400 feet in broad daylight and get the troops on the ground as quickly and as close together as possible.

Other troublesome choices also had to be made. The more heavily laden a paratrooper was with weapons and ammunition, the greater the likelihood of injury when he landed. Although Allied commanders later decided to accept the risks and load their men with nearly 100 pounds of equipment, the Germans took the opposite tack. The *Fallschirmjäger* would jump with a minimum of weapons and ammunition. Since the standard infantry rifle was too cumbersome, most of the paratroopers would carry only a pistol, a few extra clips of ammunition, and perhaps a couple of grenades. Officers and senior noncoms would carry a submachine gun short enough to be strapped to the chest. Rifles, heavy machine guns, mortars, a suitable supply of grenades, and most of the ammunition were to be dropped in canisters alongside the parachutists.

The problem, of course, was that the troopers would be badly outgunned until they recovered their regular weapons. German planners hoped to compensate for this by silently landing well-armed men in gliders just before the paratroopers. In addition to deploying a few heavy weapons and covering the descending parachutists, the glider troops would capture key enemy strongpoints, especially antiaircraft positions. The fact remained, however, that German doctrine required paratroopers to jump almost unarmed into the face of the enemy. It remained to be seen whether General Student's troops, extraordinary as they were, could get from their airplanes to their weapons and then clamp a grip on Crete.

The island's forbidding terrain gave every advantage to the defenders. Rugged mountains rose straight from the sea along the south coast and reached heights of 8,000 feet inland. Only a narrow ribbon of rolling plain along the north coast was readily accessible to planes or ships. Here were located the island's three principal towns, Canea in the west, Retimo in the center, and ancient Heraklion to the east, all connected by the island's one

Paratroopers received diving-eagle badges such as this one when they graduated from jump school. Originally bronze, the badge was made of aluminum after 1937. The oak-and-laurel wreath was plated with oxidized silver, the eagle and swastika finished in gold.

paved road. Heraklion boasted the only modern airfield and harbor facilities, although a landing strip six miles east of Retimo and an unfinished runway ten miles west of Canea, at Maleme, could handle most aircraft.

The coastal plain contained most of Crete's civilian population of nearly half a million and virtually all of its military garrison. Encamped there were more than 40,000 Allied troops. About 6,000 of them were unarmed and unorganized. The remainder included 10,000 British regulars and nearly 14,000 Commonwealth troops from Australia and New Zealand, as well as 10,000 partially equipped Greek soldiers and Cretan gendarmes. They would outnumber the nearly 25,000 Germans assigned to the invasion force, and they possessed the great advantage that, when the shooting started, they would have their feet on the ground while the assault troops dangled in the air above them.

Nor would the Germans have the benefit of surprise. Their intentions were obvious. The Allied commander, New Zealand's doughty Major General Sir Bernard Freyberg, did not know exactly when or where the Germans would attack, but British intelligence had told him that an airborne invasion was coming. There could be little doubt that the blow would fall somewhere along the north coast and that it would be aimed at an airfield.

Freyberg, a hero of Gallipoli and the Somme in World War I, had been thrust unexpectedly into command of Crete on April 30. He found in place no defense plan, no staff, and little organization, but he did the best he could. He deployed about sixty percent of his forces—principally the New Zealand and Australian units, his toughest troops, and three Greek regiments—to defend the westerly coast from Maleme to Suda Bay and his command center at Canea. The remaining forty percent—the rest of the Anzacs and Greeks, some British regulars, and Cretan gendarmes—was divided about equally between Heraklion and Retimo.

In response to a telegram from Churchill, his longtime friend and mentor, Freyberg advised London on May 5 that he was "not in the least anxious about airborne attack." But, he added that "a combination of airborne and seaborne attack is quite different." He feared such a combination and communicated his worry to his officers. As a result, during the critical first days of the battle, they would never concentrate fully on the grave danger of losing an airfield to the enemy; instead, they would be watching the empty sea over their shoulders.

On April 25, Hitler had signed Directive 28, setting in motion Student's plans for the invasion. The Führer laid down the stern proviso that the operation must be carried out by mid-May. He was intent on invading the Soviet Union in June and was determined that nothing interfere with

Vulnerable Movers of Men and Arms

The lumbering, obsolescent transport planes that bore the Wehrmacht's paratroop and air-landing battalions to Crete had seen more action than most aircraft. The Junkers 52—nicknamed *Tante Ju*, or Auntie Ju, by its crews—had inaugurated a new form of warfare in the 1930s: the rapid movement of men and matériel by air to the battlefront. Many of the Junkers towed DFS 230 A-1 assault gliders, an expendable aircraft that the Germans had first used during the invasion of the Low Countries in 1940.

In the campaign against Crete, the Ju 52s of the XI Air Corps had to operate from rudimentary Greek airfields. Each plane carried twelve to seventeen fully equipped men or four tons of supplies. Powered by three BMW 132A-3 air-cooled 725-horsepower engines, the Auntie Ju cruised at 150 miles per hour and had a range of 620 miles.

The fabric-covered DFS 230 glider jettisoned its wheeled undercarriage on takeoff and landed on a central skid. The thirty-seven-foot-long craft had an impressive seventy-two-foot wingspan. Loaded with ten men and 600 pounds of gear, it weighed only 4,600 pounds.

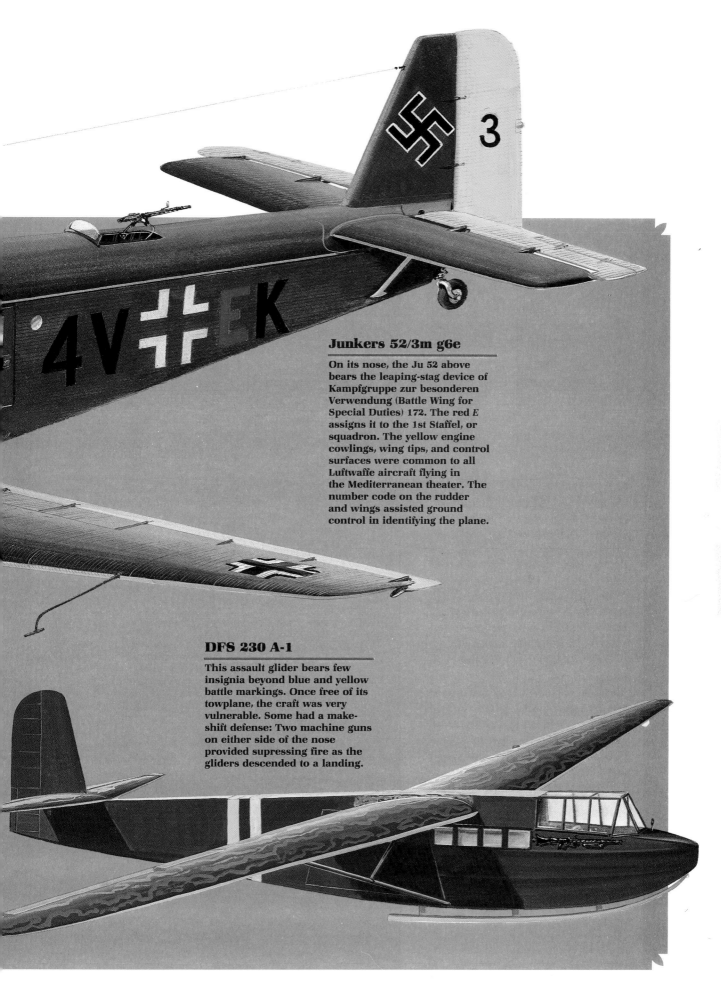

Junkers 52/3m g6e

On its nose, the Ju 52 above bears the leaping-stag device of Kampfgruppe zur besonderen Verwendung (Battle Wing for Special Duties) 172. The red *E* assigns it to the 1st Staffel, or squadron. The yellow engine cowlings, wing tips, and control surfaces were common to all Luftwaffe aircraft flying in the Mediterranean theater. The number code on the rudder and wings assisted ground control in identifying the plane.

DFS 230 A-1

This assault glider bears few insignia beyond blue and yellow battle markings. Once free of its towplane, the craft was very vulnerable. Some had a make-shift defense: Two machine guns on either side of the nose provided supressing fire as the gliders descended to a landing.

Operation Barbarossa. That left less than three weeks to mount the largest and most audacious airborne assault in history.

From all over the Reich, by train and truck, the elements of Süssmann's 7th Paratroop Division not already in Greece headed south, their mission a secret to all except the most senior officers. Meanwhile, mechanics overhauled the 500 battle-worn Ju 52s that would be needed. The "good old aunts" of the Luftwaffe had been airlifting supplies throughout the Balkans, and their airframes and engines needed attention. Quartermasters sought out the required 2.5 million gallons of aviation fuel, transported it to Greece and thence to the primitive airfields from which the invasion fleet would take off. *(See page 134.)*

While these preparations were under way, Student found to his dismay that he was not to have sole command of the invasion. Instead of reporting to Student, VIII Air Corps commander Wolfram Freiherr von Richthofen—cousin of the World War I ace and a former member of his Flying Circus—was to report as an equal subordinate to General Alexander Löhr, head of Luftflotte 4. Neither Richthofen nor Löhr was happy with Student's plans.

Student's theory of applying airborne power was to bewilder the enemy with multiple parachute drops (the commander envisioned a total of seven on Crete) and then to reinforce and consolidate. Löhr's idea was to concentrate all available forces in one massive drop on the Maleme-Canea-Suda Bay area of western Crete and then, supported by the VIII Air Corps's attack aircraft, to roll eastward.

As the originator and principal theorist of airborne assault, Student prevailed where the overall concept of the plan was concerned, but not in every detail. When Richthofen protested that he could not support so many landings simultaneously, and that the 500 Ju 52s could transport only about half the 9,500 paratroopers who were supposed to land the first day, Löhr reduced the number of drops to four, two in the morning and two in the afternoon. After a pair of paratroop regiments had been landed in the Maleme-Canea sector, the transports would return to Greece for the last two of the 7th Division's regiments. One would assault the Retimo airstrip; the other would capture the port and airfield at Heraklion. Once the paratroopers were on the ground, they would have about thirty-six hours to capture an airfield before their ammunition and supplies ran out.

After an airstrip had been secured, the second phase of the invasion could begin. The transports would deliver cargoes of heavy weapons, equipment, supplies, and roughly another 8,000 men. These units would hit the ground fully armed and organized, a powerful second thrust against defenders who by now would be confused and hard-pressed. This assignment should have gone to the other arm of Student's XI Air Corps, the

British officers reconnoiter the high ground overlooking Suda Bay, on the north coast of Crete, in November 1940. During the six months prior to the German assault, six different officers led the Allied garrison on Crete. None developed a thorough plan for the island's defense.

specially trained 22d Luftlande Division, which had followed the paratroopers in the attack on the Rotterdam airfields the previous spring. But because of the immense mobilization for the Balkan and the putative Russian campaigns, the division had been unable to extricate itself from guard duty in the Rumanian oil fields.

To take the 22d's place, Student called upon Julius Ringel's battle-wise 5th Mountain Division, which had performed admirably in Greece. Despite its lack of specific training for the task, the division's expertise in mountain warfare would suit the rugged Cretan terrain. Moreover, its compact, lightweight weapons and equipment made the division easier to transport by air. Ringel's troops, reinforced by a regiment from the 6th Mountain Division, were briefed on the seating arrangements in a Ju 52 and, more important, learned how to deploy swiftly from its belly.

The third wave of the invasion was to roll in from the sea, after the mountain troops had secured a stretch of coastline. Ringel had commandeered about sixty vessels, ranging from caïque fishing boats to small coastal freighters. This armada would land everything not transportable by plane, including horses, mules, trucks, and heavy artillery, and 6,000 additional troops. The convoy would cross the Aegean in daylight, escorted by small Italian patrol craft and under the umbrella of the Luftwaffe—but it would be frightfully vulnerable should it still be under way at night, when the Luftwaffe was little help and the Royal Navy ruled the sea.

The mission depended on support from Richthofen's VIII Air Corps. The general would have at his disposal 716 powerful aircraft: 228 Do 17, He 111,

Outfitted to Cushion the Fall

The *Fallschirmjäger*, or paratroopers, of the XI Air Corps who leaped from their transports over the island of Crete were well outfitted for the job. Each man wore a close-fitting, rubber-padded steel helmet that lacked the protruding neck-and-brow guard of the standard Wehrmacht helmet. This modification reduced the chance of a neck injury during a rough landing.

An olive green gabardine jump smock covered the paratrooper's wool uniform—a flying jacket and ski-style trousers. Kneepads and reinforced, side-laced boots cushioned his legs and ankles against the shock of hitting the ground.

German quartermasters, however, did make one serious miscalculation: Many of the parachutists found their wool clothing stifling in Crete's hot climate. They discarded their jackets and trousers and fought wearing only their shirts, drawers, and jump smocks.

Most *Fallschirmjäger* jumped into battle armed only with a semiautomatic pistol. Heavier weapons were dropped in brightly marked canisters. Selected officers and senior NCOs jumped with an MP 38 submachine gun *(below)* strapped across their chest. All ranks carried a gravity knife in a pocket on their pant leg—to free themselves if they became entangled in the parachute's shrouds.

Regulations stated that the jump smock was to be worn over the field gear *(left)*, but few paratroopers adhered to the rule. Once on the ground, the soldier picked up grenades, a gas mask, and an MP 38 ammunition pouch from the drop canisters. For combat, the helmet *(far left)* was fitted with a cloth cover in order to prevent telltale glare. Before jumping, each man packed his own RZ 20 parachute *(above)*. Hard lessons learned during the invasion of the Netherlands prompted the introduction of camouflage canopies. They reduced the trooper's chances of becoming an easy target as he shed the harness after landing.

and Ju 88 medium bombers; 205 of the deadly Ju 87 Stukas; 233 Me 109 and Me 110 fighters and fighter-bombers; and a bevy of reconnaissance planes. This formidable air fleet had swept the British Royal Air Force out of Greece. During the Allied evacuation, German fliers had relentlessly attacked the convoys, sinking dozens of vessels in a considerably more fruitful reenactment of Dunkirk. Now, during the first weeks of May 1941, the Luftwaffe roamed unopposed through the daytime skies over Crete, strafing and bombing anything that looked the least bit suspicious.

Not surprisingly, the effect on the island's defenders was profound. Most of them became loath to leave their trenches, and their commanders grew wary of shifting troops across the open countryside. But this apparent paralysis was also part bluff. In order to preserve everything he could for the invasion to come, Freyberg ordered many of his antiaircraft units to remain silent and hidden.

The morning of May 20 brought fine weather to the eastern Mediterranean. A light mist hung over the waves, but the sun would soon burn it off. Beginning at first light on half a dozen airfields in Greece, Junkers transports roared down rough runways and lifted heavily through the red dust into the sky. About sixty of the 500 Ju 52s towed gliders. These towplanes took positions in the van, while the vast fleet formed up and then banked south like a great flock of predatory birds.

The gliders bucked and jerked at the end of their ropes. Inside, it was dark and hot, and many men became airsick. But the journey was not a long one. As the fleet approached the coast of Crete, towropes were cast off and

General Kurt Student *(far right)*, overall commander of the Wehrmacht's airborne forces, confers with General Julius Ringel, whose 5th Mountain Division reinforced Student's beleaguered paratroopers on the second day of the battle.

the gliders nosed downward. The only sound was the rushing of the wind over their thin fabric skins. Behind them, the mass of aircraft, bearing about 5,500 paratroopers, descended from 5,000 feet to the drop altitude of 400 feet and throttled back to await their turn over the targets.

It was about seven o'clock, and the Allied defenders at Canea and Maleme were emerging from their dugouts after a short, vicious pounding from the air. A few minutes earlier, a score of Dornier and Heinkel bombers had thundered overhead followed by howling Stukas and fire-spitting Messerschmitts. Now the appearance of the gliders, sailing past like ravens, left little doubt about the Germans' primary objective.

Responsibility for the capture of the landing strip at Maleme fell to the largest of the 7th Division's four paratroop regiments, the Sturmregiment under Brigadier General Eugen Meindl, a rugged career officer who had distinguished himself at Narvik during the Norwegian campaign. With four battalions instead of the usual three, Meindl had about 3,000 men, including the glider detachments—still a few hundred short of the typical German infantry regiment. But in a drop, there were no rear-echelon units; the front line was all around, and even medical personnel might be called on to fight. Whatever his other military specialties, every man of the Sturmregiment was first and foremost a soldier.

Meindl's plan called for three glider detachments of some 300 men, mostly from the 1st Battalion, to prepare the way for the paratroopers. One group, under Major Walter Koch, a hero of the Belgian triumph, was supposed to seize the critical heights designated Hill 107, southeast of the airfield. Another, led by Major Franz Braun, was to capture the bridge over the dry Tavronitis River, which ran past the airfield a few hundred yards to the west. The third group, commanded by First Lieutenant Wulff von Plessen, was to take out the antiaircraft positions in the Tavronitis Delta, on the northwest edge of the airfield.

Koch's team, on Hill 107, came to immediate grief. Flying into the rising sun over ground obscured by lingering mist and smoke from the air attack,

the glider pilots misjudged their descent and were too high when they arrived over the target. They wrenched their craft downward and became widely separated. Some gliders crumpled on touchdown, killing their occupants; men in the others dashed out to discover that the terrain was far more rugged than their maps or aerial photographs had shown. The scattered units could not see one another because of the ridges and could not form up in the face of virtually point-blank enemy fire. Instead of the lightly defended hillside they had expected, the attackers found the 22d Battalion, 5th New Zealand Brigade, led by Lieut. Colonel L. W. Andrew, eagerly awaiting them in thoroughly prepared and camouflaged positions.

Within a few minutes, Koch was severely wounded in the head. Most of his men were either killed or driven back down the slopes, where the remnants rallied under their medical officer. The other two detachments arrived in somewhat better shape, although a number of their gliders crashed on landing. Braun's group seized the Tavronitis bridge (actually, his men took cover beneath it) but could make no progress toward the airfield. Plessen's troops overran the New Zealanders defending the anti-aircraft guns in the Tavronitis Delta but came under intense fire when they tried to move toward the airstrip. Both Braun and Plessen were soon killed, along with scores of their men.

Two other glider detachments, totaling about 225 men under Captain Gustav Altmann and First Lieutenant Alfred Genz, had been ordered to lead a companion paratroop action near Suda Bay that was designed to split the main force of Allied defenders. Their assault, too, was frustrated. Altmann's men tried to land near the antiaircraft guns on Akrotiri Peninsula, to the north of Suda Bay. The Germans roused a storm of flak that destroyed four gliders and scattered the rest. Once on the ground, Altmann discovered that the main Allied gun emplacement was a dummy; within hours, his entire 136-man unit was killed or taken prisoner. Meanwhile, Genz's group managed to destroy a large antiaircraft battery just south of the town of Canea, killing almost all of the 180 gunners. But the Germans were pinned down before they could reach their second objective, the main Allied radio station to the west of town.

Chaos still ruled on the ground when the transports carrying the first wave of paratroopers roared over the coast, braving the flak while desperately seeking their drop zones. "They were sitting ducks," a British gunner recalled. "You could actually see the shot breaking up the aircraft and the bodies falling out like potato sacks." Groundfire brought down several Ju 52s, but there were too many planes and too few guns for a truly effective defense. The skies above the Maleme airfield filled with hundreds of blossoming parachutes. The sight struck one New Zealand officer as "unreal,

A shirtless ground controller uses a signal flag and flare gun to launch a Ju 52 loaded with paratroopers from a Greek base. Every takeoff raised clouds of dust that spoiled the invasion timetable, delaying the planes and forcing them to ferry the second wave to Crete piecemeal.

difficult to comprehend as anything dangerous. Seen against the deep blue of the early-morning Cretan sky, through a frame of gray-green olive branches, they looked like little jerking dolls."

As planned, the drop neatly bracketed the airfield. The Sturmregiment's 2d and 4th Battalions, under Major Edgar Stentzler and Captain Walter Gericke, descended over the coast road to the west, while the 3d Battalion dropped on the road to the east. The men falling west of the field came down in a gap in the defenses. They landed virtually unopposed and quickly formed up in good order. But to the east, the 3d Battalion, led by Major Otto Scherber, parachuted directly onto strong Allied positions. Suddenly, the worst of Student's nightmares was realized: His brave battalion was literally destroyed.

"Each man dangling carried a death, his own, if not another's," wrote a New Zealand historian later. And so it was. The olive groves erupted in sheets of defensive fire that reached up and enveloped the slowly descending paratroopers. "You'd see one go limp," remembered a New Zealander, "then give a kick and kind of straighten up with a jerk and then go limp again, and you knew he was done for." Other Germans were snagged on trees or slammed sickeningly onto the rocks lining the coast. The men who landed safely were instantly pinned down and unable to reach their weapons canisters, many of which had fallen into Allied hands anyway. With only their pistols and a few submachine guns, they were no match for the enemy's rifles, mortars, and machine guns.

Hundreds of men dropped within the area defended by the New Zealand 23d Battalion, whose colonel shot five paratroopers. A New Zealand platoon leader hunting down paratroopers lost two of his men but returned with the identification disks from twenty-nine German bodies. At the village of Modhion, the New Zealand lieutenant in charge of a field punishment center took it upon himself to release sixty hard-case inmates—who celebrated their unexpected freedom by killing 110 Germans. One German company commander carried a roll-call roster listing 126 names; within two hours, 112 of the men on the list had been slain. Every officer in the 3d Battalion was either killed or wounded. A few noncoms remained to rally small groups of agonized men who crouched woefully in the hollows, without water in the awful heat, praying for nightfall.

Of the 600 men who had jumped with Major Scherber, nearly 400 died, including Scherber himself. The initial attack on Maleme from the east had ended in calamity. Throughout the struggle, here as elsewhere, squadrons of Luftwaffe bombers and fighters circled ominously overhead. But it was impossible for them to discern friend from foe in the confused fighting. Thus for a time, the outcome was beyond the influence of air power.

Gliders that brought Major Franz Braun's assault group to Crete lie on the broken terrain where they landed on May 20. The pilots touched down within a few hundred yards of their target—a bridge over the Tavronitis riverbed—which Braun's troops secured under heavy fire.

General Meindl had parachuted onto the battlefield at half past eight, landing to the west, where the 2d and 4th Battalions were hotly engaged with the New Zealanders stationed on Hill 107 and around the airfield. He immediately realized that the 1st Battalion's glider assaults had failed, and it soon became apparent that something had gone terribly wrong for Scherber's 3d Battalion to the east. Already, nearly half of Meindl's regiment was gone. If he were to take the Maleme airfield, it would have to be from the west, with his 2d and 4th Battalions. If he failed, the rest of his force would be wiped out as well.

Meindl quickly reorganized his troops west of the airfield into two assault groups. He ordered elements of the 4th Battalion, under Captain Gericke, to strike across the Tavronitis bridge toward the airfield. Major Stentzler and two companies of the 2d Battalion were to traverse the dry riverbed south of the bridge and work around Hill 107 for an attack up its southern slope. Both groups immediately ran into searing fire from the determined New Zealanders.

Meindl still hoped that Koch might have gained a toehold on Hill 107, and he thought to wave aloft a signal flag. As he rose from cover, a New Zealand sharpshooter put a bullet in the raised hand. A moment later, the general went down with a machine-gun slug in his chest. Though seriously wounded, he remained conscious and in command.

Under Gericke, the 4th Battalion charged the entrenched Allies again and again. They made progress, but it was costly and came only after protracted fighting, often hand-to-hand. Some of the enemy hurled handmade grenades fashioned from jam tins filled with concrete and plugs of gelatin

dynamite—crude but effective. In the 100-degree heat, the heavy paratroop uniforms clung like sodden blankets to the men's bodies, and many of the paras, seeking relief, slashed off the trouser legs or stripped to their jump smocks. Despite rapidly mounting casualties, Gericke's men by late afternoon had secured part of the airfield and established a strong bridgehead between the field and the north face of Hill 107. But Stentzler's 2d Battalion companies were unable to make much headway against the positions along the south slope of the hill. And possession of part of the airfield, even all of it, would mean little if the New Zealanders remained on Hill 107, where they could train their guns on the runways. Meindl, running out of daylight, prepared his men for a last, desperate night assault on the hill.

He did not know it, but the New Zealanders' situation was equally dire. All day, Colonel Andrew and his men had held off furious attacks. By nightfall, Andrew had sacrificed nearly half his battalion, committed all his reserves, and lost contact with three of his companies. His wire communications had been destroyed in the initial bombing, his radio batteries were almost dead, and he had been reduced to using lights, flares, and runners to gather information and send for help.

Aware how important it was that he hold his position, he urgently requested reinforcements from the other battalions of the 5th New Zealand Brigade, which had done little except guard the beaches since wiping out Meindl's 3d Battalion that morning. But the brigade commander, Brigadier James Hargest, was unwilling to move, largely because his men had captured a German map that showed enemy drop zones all across his sector. Fearing that more paratroopers were on the way, Hargest insisted on holding his men in place rather than sliding west to counter the Germans already on the ground. In desperation, Andrew decided to attempt a counterattack spearheaded by two heavy Matilda tanks that he had kept concealed in an almond grove.

Leading all the infantry Andrew could spare—scarcely twenty men—the tanks churned toward the Tavronitis River, where Captain Gericke and his men were positioned just east of the bridge. This was a bad moment for the Germans. Without weapons that could penetrate such thick armor, the paratroopers feared a tank attack more than anything else. Gericke later confessed that "panic threatened to break out" when the men saw their small-arms fire pinging harmlessly off the Matildas' tough metal hides. But the attack came to naught. Inexplicably, the ammunition would not fit the cannon in the lead tank, and the New Zealand crew hastily abandoned it. The second tank rolled down the bank into the riverbed and turned toward the sea, rumbling under the bridge and firing in every direction. But 200 yards downstream, the behemoth became stuck among huge river boul-

ders. The crew bailed out into a storm of fire sweeping their accompanying infantry. Only a lucky few returned to their mates east of the airfield.

While Meindl and his Sturmregiment struggled to survive, a roughly equivalent force, consisting of the 3d Paratroop Regiment and the division's Engineer Battalion, was dropped near Canea, about seven miles east of Maleme. Assuming that the glider troops had done their job, the regiment expected to overwhelm the Allied command center and prevent reinforcement of the troops defending the airfield. Its drop zone extended southwest from the vicinity of the town of Galatas down along a shallow valley to a village called Alikianou.

So critical was this part of the invasion plan that General Süssmann, the 7th Division commander, intended to direct it from the battlefield. But disaster struck even before the regiment reached Crete. Shortly after takeoff, the glider carrying Süssmann suddenly lost its wings. The fuselage plunged straight down, carrying the general to his death on the rocky island of Aegina. No one was ever certain what caused the accident, but it is likely that an overtaking He 111 bomber passed so close that the glider's towrope broke in the bomber's slipstream, causing the glider to pitch up violently and overstressing its fragile wings. Command of the Galatas operation passed to the 3d Regiment's Colonel Richard Heidrich, a single-minded man whose entire adult life had been devoted to the military.

The drop turned out to be as difficult as the Sturmregiment's ordeal at Maleme. The 1st Battalion landed more or less where it was supposed to, in a shallow, populated valley dominated by an unused prison building, and met little initial opposition. Its captain, a young baron named Friedrich-August von der Heydte, recalled the scene: "I could see people in the streets staring up at us, others running away and disappearing into doorways. The shadows of our planes swept like ghostly hands over the sun-drenched white houses. On every side during the drop, parachutes surrounded me, but on landing I was absolutely alone. It is a strange feeling to be dropped suddenly into an alien land with orders to conquer it. Every tree, every bush, every blade of grass holds its secret." Baron Heydte quickly collected his men, and his forward elements probed northward toward Canea. But heavy fire from British and Greek units soon pinned them down.

The 2d and 3d Battalions were far less fortunate. The 2d Battalion dropped on the northern slopes of the valley, in the olive groves near Galatas. The 10th New Zealand Brigade was waiting for them, and the paratroopers took heavy casualties from the moment they left their planes. Only four of the dozen men in Sergeant Major Karl Neuhoff's transport reached the ground unhurt. He estimated that barely 350 of the battalion's

"Like autumn leaves, drifting down," in the words of a German officer, canopies bearing the 3d Paratroop Regiment descend on

Crete. Although maps described its landing area south of Galatas as a plateau, the regiment instead dropped into a shallow valley.

A parachute serves as a shroud for a German trooper who landed in an olive tree and was killed before he could extricate himself from his harness.

550 men survived the first few minutes of swirling combat. At one point, a startled German private found himself in sole possession of the 10th New Zealand's headquarters. Its colonel was isolated in a nearby hedge. This triumph of airborne surprise was only momentary. The colonel crept around back, shot the paratrooper, and regained his command post.

To the east, the 3d Battalion had been widely scattered during the drop and was spread over a distance of two miles. Some of the men linked up with Heydte's 1st Battalion, but the rest were cut off and decimated by nightfall. Equally unfortunate was the Engineer Battalion, which dropped to the southwest—into the guns of a Greek regiment and local Cretan irregulars who had helped themselves to the paratroopers' weapons canisters. The Greeks and Cretans threw themselves on the invaders with a fury, and the next day more than 100 German bodies were found in one small area. Most members of the divisional headquarters staff also came to a quick end when their gliders crashed near the south tip of the valley.

Colonel Heidrich struggled to restore cohesion to his badly mauled units. After consolidating his position around the prison buildings in the middle of the valley, he and his officers labored into the early afternoon, gathering the survivors of the morning's debacle. By midafternoon, he had at his disposal scarcely 1,000 of his original 3,000 men. With this drastically reduced force, he would have to defend his positions and drive to the northeast, toward Canea and Suda Bay. First, however, he had to capture the high ground around Galatas on his left flank. His initial attack—400 men sent against Allied emplacements on a hill just south of Galatas—was driven back. A second, reinforced assault in the early evening succeeded.

The German victory was short-lived, however. That night, two Allied companies supported by three light tanks advanced against the lightly armed paratroopers. Unnerved by the armor, the Germans fled into the valley after a brief fight. Now, with time working against him and no reinforcements in the offing, Heidrich radioed Student at his Athens headquarters for permission to lead the remnant of his force west in order to join the Sturmregiment at Maleme. Student ordered him to close ranks and hang on. Instead of sweeping through the center of the Allied defenses, the 3d Regiment in Prison Valley was stalled and on the defensive. It had nevertheless succeeded in one major objective: to hold the opposing troops away from the fight for Maleme. And now the fighting force had company to the east as well. The rest of the 7th Division was on the ground at Retimo and Heraklion—although these regiments, too, were hung up and fighting for their lives.

Confusion had ruled the Greek airfields from the moment the first transports returned to fetch the second wave of paratroopers. From midday onward, clouds of dust obscured the ground. All semblance of squadron discipline was lost as pilots circled for an hour or more before groping their way to individual landings. Runway collisions took a greater toll of Ju 52s than all the Allied guns on Crete. In the murk and noise, timetables fell into shambles while ground crews worked frantically to refuel the planes with hand pumps and to match transports with the units assigned to them.

The plan had called for the second wave to hit Crete at one o'clock and for all 3,500 paratroopers to be on the ground shortly thereafter. But scarcely any of the transports arrived on time, and some squadrons straggled over their drop zones as much as three hours late. What was to be a swift, surgical insertion preceded by intense bombing became an interminable horror, with the enemy below fully alerted and ardently waiting.

The force assigned to capture the landing strip east of Retimo was the smallest of the four invasion commands. It consisted of 1,500 men, primarily two reinforced battalions of the 2d Paratroop Regiment under Colonel Alfred Sturm, a cocksure veteran of Holland and the Corinth Canal. The command was organized in three groups, one of which was ordered to drop about a mile east of Retimo and capture the town. A second group was to come down just east of the landing strip and quickly seize it. The third and smallest group, comprising only the headquarters company and Colonel Sturm, was to land along the coast between the two forces to coordinate the attacks.

To Sturm's dismay, many of his transports were shot down before they could disgorge their men. Seven planes crashed on the beach, and others

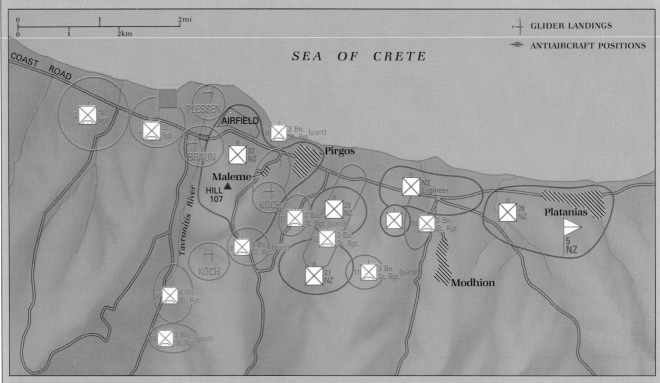

GLIDER LANDINGS

ANTIAIRCRAFT POSITIONS

0 1 2mi
0 1 2km

SEA OF CRETE

COAST ROAD

PLESSEN

AIRFIELD

2 | St. Rgt.

4 | St. Rgt.

3 Bn. (part) St. Rgt.

BRAUN

22 | NZ

Pirgos

Maleme

HILL 107

KOCH

Tavronitis River

3 Bn. St. Rgt. (part)

23 | NZ

NZ Engineer

3 Bn. St. Rgt. (part)

3 Bn. St. Rgt.

28 | NZ

Platanias

5 NZ

KOCH

9 | 3 Bn. St. Rgt. (part)

21 | NZ

3 Bn. St. Rgt. (part)

10 |

Modhion

16 | Bn. St. Rgt.

3 Bn. St. Rgt. (part)

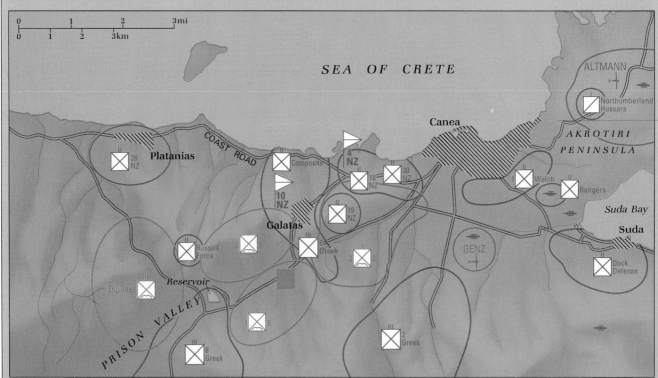

0 1 2 3mi
0 1 2 3km

SEA OF CRETE

ALTMANN

Canea

Northumberland Hussars

AKROTIRI PENINSULA

28 | NZ

Platanias

COAST ROAD

Composite

4 NZ

18 | NZ

20 | NZ

Welch

Rangers

10 NZ

19 | NZ

Suda Bay

Suda

Galatas

Greek

GENZ

Dock Defense

Russell Force

2 | 3

3

Engineer

Reservoir

3

PRISON VALLEY

8 Greek

2 Greek

These maps show the airborne landings on the western end of the island of Crete during the morning of May 20, 1941. German drop zones are shown in red, Allied defensive positions in blue. Glider assaults that preceded the paratroopers were to seize selected targets and neutralize Allied antiaircraft batteries. At Maleme (*top*), the German plan called for Brigadier General Eugen Meindl's Sturmregiment (St.Rgt.) to come down all around the airstrip and capture it in a converging attack. In the Canea-Galatas area (*bottom*), Colonel Richard Heidrich's 3d Regiment was to overrun the Allied command center and prevent the troops there from reinforcing the defenders of the landing fields at Maleme to the east and Retimo to the west.

wobbled out to sea trailing smoke and flame. The drop itself was long and costly, and troops were scattered all over the countryside. Sturm was captured almost immediately after landing, his headquarters company virtually wiped out. The eastern group was dispersed over five miles, and the elements closest to the airfield quickly became engaged with its defenders. Despite fearful casualties, these paratroopers eventually drove an Australian unit from a hill overlooking the landing strip. Meanwhile, the force attacking Retimo lost almost half its number during the drop. The few hundred survivors regrouped and headed for the town, where they set up a roadblock to stymie Allied reinforcements from Canea. But overall, the operation could not be deemed a success.

The fourth and final paratroop attack was launched against the harbor and airfield at Heraklion, the ancient Minoan port a few miles north of the ruins of Knossos. Although its landing facilities were the best on Crete,

Paratroopers regroup in an olive grove after retrieving the arms and ammunition that were dropped with their squad. Although the weapons containers were brightly marked, finding them in strange country under hostile fire was difficult.

Heraklion was nevertheless allotted a smaller invasion force because of its distant location. The attack would be carried out by 2,000 men in three battalions of the 1st Paratroop Regiment, along with the 2d Battalion of the 2d Regiment, all commanded by Colonel Bruno Bräuer, a veteran of the First World War and former security policeman who had been one of the first paratroop officers.

This drop, like the others, became a horror. The Australian defenders held their antiaircraft fire until the planes were almost overhead, then the Bofors 40-mm pompoms opened up. Fifteen transports crashed in the hail of exploding shells. As desperate paratroopers jumped from one burning Ju 52, each opening parachute in succession blossomed orange when touched by the trailing fire, then vanished in a puff of smoke, casting the Germans to their deaths. When another shot-up transport, losing its fight to maintain altitude, expelled its troops, every soldier hit the ground before his chute could open. A British officer watched one paratrooper descend on top of his company headquarters. "When he was about ten feet from the ground, seven or eight of our Tigers, each with bayonet fixed, rose and approached him. That was the first time I had heard a man scream with fright." Other Germans defiantly sprayed fire from their submachine guns as they came down. Still others arrived with their hands up in a sign of surrender, only to hurl grenades once on the ground.

The drop lasted for three hours, until half past seven. By then, several hundred paratroopers had died, and the Allies were attacking the units that had managed to form up. One Australian company killed ninety Germans while losing only three of its own men.

The 3d Battalion, entrusted with the capture of Heraklion, escaped the landing with light casualties but suffered terribly during repeated assaults against the Greeks guarding their objective. That evening, the paratroopers penetrated the north and west gates of the walled city and by half past ten reached the harbor, but they were driven out after bitter fighting. The paratroopers had been told that the Cretans would welcome them, but the intelligence proved faulty. At Heraklion, as in other towns, the inhabitants fought ferociously; shots, shouts, and screams echoed far into the night.

At the airfield, the Australians and British swiftly destroyed the 2d Battalion, which had landed in two groups. Only one officer and 60 men survived from the eastern companies; the western companies were all but wiped out within twenty minutes. Those who remained "succumbed to the immediate attack of several light and medium tanks," as a German battle report put it. Inside of an hour, 12 officers and 300 men of the battalion were dead, another 8 officers and 100 men were wounded, and fewer than 100 paratroopers remained at large and fit to fight.

Three paratroopers hug the ground as a mortar shell explodes in front of them. In the first two days' fighting, the Germans had relatively few heavy weapons and could not engage the Allies with equal firepower.

Colonel Bräuer and elements of his 1st Battalion had landed east of the airfield, but almost five miles from their objective, and it took them until midnight to join the remnant of the 2d Battalion on the high ground overlooking the airfield. When Bräuer finally established contact with the remainder of his regiment, he could only tell them to renew their attacks at dawn with whatever force they had left.

The first day of Crete had cost General Student thousands of his elite troops, nearly one-third of the 7th Division, and nowhere had the invaders achieved their objective. The Allies had suffered considerably fewer casualties, but no one had ever fought a battle like this, and the seemingly inexhaustible battalions descending from the sky in malevolent clouds exerted a smothering effect on the defenders. At his command post, General Freyberg and his officers did not know how many more German paratroop units might appear in the morning. And they still feared an invasion from the sea. At ten that night, Freyberg sent a message to Cairo for General Sir Archibald Wavell, commander in chief of British forces in the Middle East. "Today has been a hard one," Freyberg reported. "So far, I believe we hold the aerodromes at Maleme, Heraklion, Retimo, and the two harbors. Margin by which we hold them is a bare one, and it would be wrong of me to paint an optimistic picture."

In Athens, Kurt Student paced his headquarters on the second floor of the Hôtel Grande-Bretagne, the irony of whose name—the Hotel Great Britain—did not escape anyone. Through the night of May 20, Student agonized over the reports from Crete. Despite the confusion of combat, it was clear that a debacle was in the making: Four of his battalions, including his

glider troops, had been shattered. The pride of the German Wehrmacht lay dead or writhing in pain among the olive groves and sweet-smelling jasmine and mimosa of Crete. And despite the troopers' reckless gallantry, no airfield was yet available for the landing of the mountain troops or desperately needed ammunition and supplies. It seemed likely that a determined Allied counterattack would annihilate the invasion force.

General Löhr, who had yielded his invasion plan to Student's, and General Richthofen, who had fought with Student over it, could scarcely contain their hostility: What did Student propose now? Should they abandon the invasion before losing more troops, and if not, what then? Student went to his room, alone, to try to find some answers. Later, all he remembered thinking was "If only we can get through this night."

So thought every soldier on Crete, and not one more than New Zealand's Lieut. Colonel Andrew, still clinging to Hill 107 overlooking the airfield at Maleme. As he examined his options, Andrew arrived at a fateful decision.

Members of a small German unit, finding temporary shelter in a dry streambed shielded by a weed-choked embankment, take turns resting and watching before they resume the advance.

The Second Wave of Landings

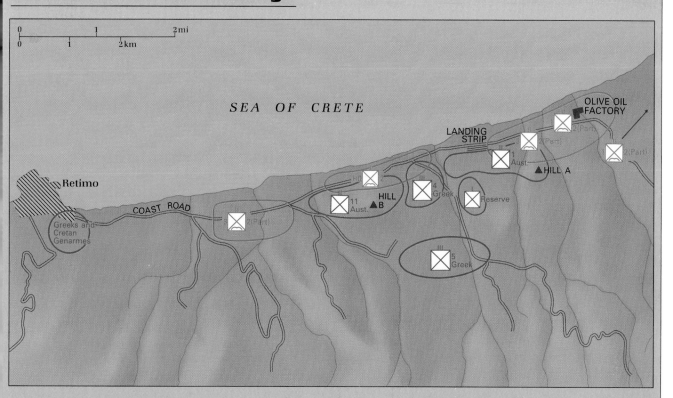

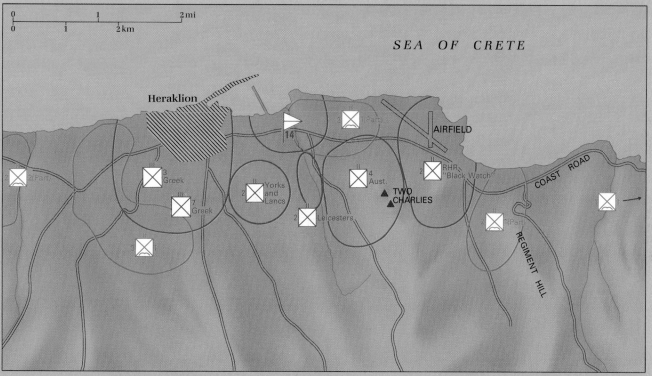

Around three in the afternoon, after a two-hour delay, the bulk of the 2d Paratroop Regiment, led by Colonel Alfred Sturm, began landing at Retimo *(top)*. Sturm had divided the force—about 1,500 strong—into three units. One was to seize the airstrip, another was to capture the town, and the third was to set up a command post. About the same time, Colonel Bruno Bräuer and 2,000 men of the 1st Paratroop Regiment, augmented by units of the 2d, jumped over Heraklion *(bottom)*. Part of the command was to storm the harbor, the rest was to capture the airport. Both operations met with disaster. Instead of a concentrated attack, the men were dropped over several hours, and many were widely dispersed. Scores were killed within minutes of jumping; one of Bräuer's battalions landed directly on top of Allied positions and was all but destroyed.

Denied reinforcements by his brigade commander and disheartened by the failure of his armored counterattack, Andrew became convinced that his 22d Battalion would soon be overrun. The Germans held the western edge of the airfield and the northwest shoulder of the hill. They had cut off and, Andrew thought, probably destroyed three forward companies of New Zealanders. Ominous patrols of another German force were already probing the hill's southern flank. At dawn, Andrew believed, his besieged New Zealanders would face renewed attacks not only from the front and rear, but from the sky, as the Luftwaffe fliers sorted out the positions and resumed strafing and bombing. Reluctantly, Andrew decided that he had no choice but to retreat.

In fact, the New Zealanders' situation was better than Andrew thought. His companies, though isolated and out of touch, were dug in, fighting hard, and in reasonably good spirits. General Hargest had changed his mind and dispatched reinforcements. Meanwhile, the survivors of Meindl's Sturmregiment were exhausted, thirsty, and disheartened; no more than 1,000 of the original 3,000 remained in action. The wounded German general himself was in bad shape, his chest slowly filling with blood. Later analysis suggested that a spirited New Zealand counterattack would have driven the paratroopers from the flank of Hill 107 and the airfield. But when Andrew radioed Hargest that he might have to withdraw, his commander offered no encouragement. Replied Hargest, "If you must, you must."

In the last hour before dawn, two small parties of Germans dragged themselves up for a last attempt to take the hill from two sides. First Lieutenant Horst Trebes led one party, the survivors of Braun's group and the 3d Battalion. The chief regimental surgeon, Dr. Heinrich Neumann, directed the other. He had assumed command of Koch's group when all other senior officers were put out of action. Only silence greeted Neumann and his men as they cautiously clambered up the rocky slope littered with their dead comrades. They reached the first line of entrenchments and found it empty. Then they knew. Within minutes, the parties from north and south met at the summit, scarcely able to believe their good fortune. Down below, Major Stentzler and Captain Gericke, with what was left of the 2d and 4th Battalions, resumed their penetrations and realized that the killing machine-gun fire had ceased. Hill 107 was quiet.

The Germans on the hill had not been celebrating long when, just after dawn, a lone Ju 52 swept out of the north, circled the hill, and landed on the hard beach just beyond the airfield. The Junkers carried a staff aide to Student who had come on the general's orders to assess the situation at Maleme. It was the best thing the haggard Student could think to do. He had sent similar probes to overfly Heraklion and Retimo, but his strongest

After flinging their hand grenades, two paratroopers rush an Allied position. Lacking artillery support, the assault troops had to rely on such basic infantry tactics to root out the enemy.

hope rested with the Sturmregiment and Maleme. The staff officer remained for only a few minutes—long enough to unload some ammunition and confer with the gravely wounded Meindl. He did not have time to confirm that Hill 107 had, in some miraculous fashion, fallen into German hands. But his safe landing was sufficiently revealing; only sporadic artillery and small-arms fire came from the eastern edge of the airfield. He took off with the important information for his general that "the western edge of the airfield lies in dead ground," meaning under German control.

While he waited for the first-hand report, Student remained deep in thought. He wanted to continue the operation, and that required reinforcing the embattled paratroopers at Maleme. The question was how. Ringel's 5th Mountain Division was on alert, ready to go, yet Student kept postponing their jump-off, half an hour at a time. At length, Richthofen burst out in frustration, "Blood flows and hours pass uselessly by!" But not

until his aide reported that landing at Maleme would be "hard but feasible" did Student make his command decision—to stake everything on a renewed assault at Maleme.

His first step was to dispatch six transports loaded with precious supplies and ammunition. To increase their chances of landing safely, the planes touched down on the beach northwest of the airfield, beyond the range of Allied guns. A short time later, about 350 paratroopers (not deployed because of transport difficulties the day before) were dropped in the safe zone west of the Tavronitis. All through the morning and into the afternoon of May 21, the reinforced Germans slugged it out with a strong Allied rear guard for control of the area east of the airfield. Progress was slow and costly, and at nightfall a hail of fire from two companies of dug-in New Zealanders halted the paratroopers' advance.

In the meantime, two more landings took place. About half past three,

Beyond a crude wheelbarrow, smoke from Ju 52s set on fire by British shells blackens the sky over the unfinished Maleme airstrip on the battle's second day. The shelling destroyed a dozen planes, but by late that night, Germans controlled the field.

two companies left behind in the assault on Heraklion jumped east of the Maleme field, where the Sturmregiment's 3d Battalion had been slaughtered the day before. They, too, were cut to pieces. One officer and eighty men managed to fight west to the German positions. Then, sometime around five o'clock, the sky filled once more with aircraft, and a swarm of Ju 52s thundered in at wavetop level from the north, making straight-in landing runs on the Maleme field. This was Student's gamble; whether the airfield was secure or not, these planes were going to land with the first contingent of mountain troops—a full battalion and the headquarters staff of the 100th Mountain Regiment, a total of nearly 800 men. On board one of the last planes was the hard-bitten, irascible Colonel Bernhard Ramcke, coming to replace Meindl as commander of the invasion forces in western Crete. The orders he carried were simple: Drive east until all threats to the landing operations are eliminated. But first he had to get on the ground. As the first transports thumped down, Allied artillery pounded the runway. Some Ju 52s burst into flames, other had their wings sheared off. Still others struck shell craters and their landing gear collapsed. Germans on the ground used a captured British vehicle to drag wreckage out of the way of incoming aircraft, and the hulks of eighty Ju 52s soon lined the runway.

On one transport, Kurt Meyer, a German war correspondent, recorded his landing: "The lookouts on each side sweep back the great doors so that the wind almost throws us from our seats. At half the height of the mountains, we follow the line of surf. Machine-gun tracers dance below us and over the waves. Impossible to land. Once more, we turn back over the water. Heavy artillery fire covers the landing ground. Brown fountains of earth leap up and shower the machines that have already landed. Now the pilot comes in again. This time, he makes the attempt along the strip of shore of Maleme Bay. All the surface is irregular. Broad strips of sand cut through by rivulets. Between them lie thick clumps of weeds and smashed machines. We can't get down here. Shall we have another go on the landing strip? Out of the question. Obstacles everywhere. Our pilot turns away. He's got to land. The devil take this Crete!

"Hello, now we've caught it! Machine-gun bullets tear through the right wing. The pilot grits his teeth. Suddenly, there leaps before us a vineyard. We strike the ground and bounce. One wing grinds into the sand and tears the machine half around. Men, packs, boxes, ammunition are flung forward. Nothing we try to hold supports us. At last, we come to a standstill, the machine standing half on its head."

Such headlong defiance of caution could not be quenched for long. By evening, the bulk of a mountain battalion was on the ground and had secured the airfield. The Germans now held the key to victory. ✚

At an airfield in Greece, ground crews hand-pump fuel into Ju 52s of the invasion fleet. The leaping-stag emblem on their nose

A Miracle of Mobilization

Hitler's April decree that the assault on Crete begin by the middle of May presented the Wehrmacht with a nearly impossible challenge: to mobilize the necessary men and matériel in a matter of days. The XI Air Corps, chosen to carry the brunt of the operation, was scattered across Europe. Three of its four paratroop regiments had to travel by train from Germany to Rumania, then by truck over 1,000 miles of wretched roads to southern Greece. The corps's 22d Air-Landing Division, which had been guarding oil fields in Rumania, lacked transport south, and the 5th Mountain Division, already in Greece, had to replace it. By May 14, nearly 25,000 troops had somehow been assembled.

The workhorse Ju 52s that would tow gliders and ferry troops to Crete were worn out after the Balkans campaign; hundreds of the trimotor planes had to be overhauled at service centers in Germany, Czechoslovakia, and Austria. By May 15, the refurbished Ju 52s had reached their jumping-off points, little-used airfields that were scraggly strips of sand. One commander derided them as "nothing but deserts" and predicted that heavily laden aircraft "will sink in them up to their axles." Indeed, in practice takeoffs, the transports churned up clouds of dust so thick they took a quarter of an hour to settle.

Because the railroads were bad and the roads worse, most invasion supplies had to come south on ships sailing the Adriatic from Trieste to the Greek ports of Piraeus and Corinth. Hampered by Allied mines and submarines, the ships had only begun to arrive on May 17, the intended D-day, forcing a twenty-four-hour postponement. Aviation fuel was also in short supply. In the Corinth Canal, a wrecked bridge blocked a tanker carrying 650,000 gallons that the Ju 52s needed just to launch the invasion. Navy divers flew from Germany to remove the debris, but the launch date had to be delayed again, to May 20. Even then, the tasks of unloading the volatile gasoline into forty-five-gallon drums, trucking it to the remote airfields, and fueling the first planes bound for Crete were completed only hours before the invasion was to begin.

dentifies the planes as part of Battle Wing for Special Duties 172.

Missions Organized in the Dark

Disorder reigned at darkened airfields in the early hours of May 20, as the men of the XI Air Corps arrived to begin their mission. Units groped to find their assigned aircraft as the ear-pounding roar of engines revving drowned out voices, and whirling propellers kicked up huge columns of powdery dust, blinding the soldiers and threatening to clog the engines. Once assembled and suited up, the German paratroopers were guided to their planes by flashlight beams. Only after climbing aboard did the invaders learn their destination.

Before enplaning, paratroopers check their gear and strap on parachutes and kneepads. Each man carried amphetamine tablets to combat fatigue and a two-day supply of rations that included chocolate, sugar, bread, and thirst-quenching lozenges.

From a squatting position with feet spread, a paratrooper lunges headfirst into space. As he falls, a static line, connecting his harness to a cable running the length of the fuselage inside the plane, will pull taut to open his parachute and then snap free.

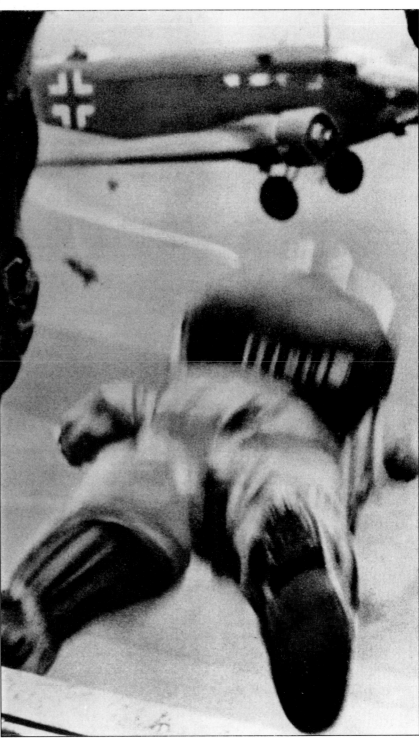

A Tense Wait for the Infantry

At the Tanagra airfield, the 100th Regiment of the 5th Mountain Division finally took off for Crete at three o'clock on May 21, after a twelve-hour delay caused by uncertain battle conditions on the island. It had been a tense wait for the alpine troops, who had just arrived in southern Greece after a long march south through the Balkan peninsula—a march interrupted by hard fighting at the Metaxas Line.

Crete's rugged terrain did not worry them, but the mountaineers were apprehensive about their first airlift into a combat zone where they would be instantly exposed to dangerous enemy fire.

Sun-parched mountain troops wait to board their transports. They carried motorcycles and other heavy equipment with them.

Wearing life vests and clutching their rifles, the men take their places in the plane's belly, six on each side.

As Crete comes into view, two soldiers peer through their plane's windows for signs of fighting below.

Entering the "Gates of Hell"

Nothing could have prepared the battle-seasoned Germans for their fiery reception on the island of Crete. Antiaircraft guns hammered their low-flying transports at close range. Groundfire raked those troopers who managed to jump, killing scores of them during the fifteen-second eternity it took to reach the ground. The men of the 5th Mountain Division, tumbling dizzy and bruised from their transports into a landscape strewn with dead bodies and wrecked planes, were met by a barrage of scathing machine-gun fire. Their commander, General Julius Ringel, referred to it as "entering the Gates of Hell."

Mountain troops *(right)* crouch behind a Ju 52 at the Maleme airfield. The unpaved strip was so small that General Kurt Student, their commander, called it a "little red tennis court."

Paratroopers from a Ju 52 float to the ground as a second transport hurtles earthward. Nearly half the Ju 52 fleet was damaged or destroyed in the campaign.

A Costly Triumph

he young fighting men of General Julius Ringel's 5th Mountain Division were mostly from the alpine regions of Germany and Austria. When they heard that part of the division was slated to arrive in Crete by sea, they were excited and amused. An Aegean cruise would be an appealing novelty, and a wag among them quickly renamed their unit the "5th Air-Landing Naval Mountain Division." Those chosen for the amphibious operation had no idea that the Greek sailing caïques and rusty tramps assembled to carry them would stink of fish and filthy bilges, that the vessels would pitch and roll in any sea, that the convoy could barely sustain four knots of speed, and that the fearsome British navy was expecting them and would come hunting. As the German troops gradually learned these things, apprehension overwhelmed anticipation.

Nevertheless, the die had been cast. The 1st Battalion of the 100th Mountain Regiment had been inserted by air, but after two days of fighting, the Wehrmacht's hold on the airfield at Maleme remained tenuous. The bloodied remnants of the Sturmregiment had greeted the arrival of their new commander, Colonel Bernhard Ramcke, with joy and relief. "Praise God, the colonel is here!" shouted one officer as he and others ran up to their scrappy little instructor from parachute school. Ramcke had rallied his battered paratroopers at the airfield and then ordered the newly arrived mountain battalion, one of three in Colonel Willibald Utz's 100th Mountain Regiment, to prepare for a southward flanking movement around the enemy forces east of the field. As dusk settled over Maleme on May 21, little more than 1,800 Germans were fit for action; the Allies had 7,000 trained infantrymen and another 6,000 ancillary troops within ten miles.

That evening in Athens, preparing to join his men, the 5th Division's commander was worried. "The second day's combat has left the decision on a knife edge," wrote General Ringel. "A British counterattack in concentrated force would require a life-and-death effort on the part of every German." It was imperative that strong reinforcements with heavy weapons be sent in by sea that very night.

Indeed, the plan had been to land a first wave of seaborne troops under

Helmets off and sweating, German alpine soldiers pursue the Allies retreating eastward. The infusion of these tough, well-equipped troops on the second day of fighting in Crete turned the tide in the Germans' favor.

the umbrella of the Luftwaffe much earlier in the day, and a flotilla of twenty-five lumbering vessels bearing 2,331 men, including the 3d Battalion of the 100th Mountain Regiment, some paratroopers, and assorted other units, had left the island of Melos on the night of May 20. For escort, they had only the Italian corvette *Lupo*. The Germans had argued for a major sortie by the Italian fleet to draw the Royal Navy from Crete, but the Italians had declined. Instead, the Germans hoped to deceive the British by filling the airwaves with fake radio transmissions.

Struggling against adverse winds, the convoy of caïques had the distant mountains of Crete in sight as the sun rose on May 21. But when the Luftwaffe reported that enemy warships were approaching, the convoy

German soldiers grin confidently from the crowded deck of a Greek caïque, one of sixty-three vessels commandeered to ferry them to Crete. The Germans organized the makeshift flotillas because the Luftwaffe did not have the planes to build up forces rapidly or transport heavy weapons and equipment.

returned to the protection of the Greek islands. When it set forth again six hours later, it had lost any chance of reaching Crete during daylight hours, when the Luftwaffe could protect it. Shortly before midnight, the fleet was still eighteen miles off the landing beaches just west of Maleme. On board the caïques, unit leaders checked their landing assignments and life rafts were inflated. The mountaineers removed their heavy shoes and donned flotation jackets. Signal pistols were made ready. On shore, beach guides with their electric beacons waited anxiously.

Without warning, disaster struck. The night was suddenly filled with stabbing searchlight beams, thrumming engines, and thundering cannon. The Royal Navy—three cruisers and four destroyers—was into the convoy like a wolf among sheep.

Since the start of the invasion, elements of the British Mediterranean Fleet, under Admiral Sir Andrew Cunningham, had been patrolling the nighttime sea lanes off the Cretan north coast in prospect of just such a move. Each dawn, the navy had retired south and west to take themselves beyond the range of German planes based in Greece. Yet air attacks had already sunk the British destroyer *Juno* and damaged the cruiser *Ajax*. That afternoon, an RAF reconnaissance plane had spotted the squadron of heavily laden caïques. Now, in the night, the navy's hour had arrived.

At the first flash of searchlights, the caïques cut their engines and struck their sails, hoping that silence and a low profile would hide them. "To us, the searchlights appear like fingers of death," a mountain trooper wrote. "Sharply cut against the darkness, they grope blindly here and there over the water. For a moment, they touch our mast tips in brilliant light, then wander on. Are we too small to be seen?" Under most circumstances, perhaps, but not when the hunters also had radar. From his drifting boat, the soldier stared up in horror. "The thing is right in front of us. A dark shadow, high as a church tower. The searchlights flash out again, drenching our tiny vessel in light as bright as day. 'Everybody overboard!' As we leap into the water, the first salvos crash into us like a tempest, sending showers of wood and debris about our ears."

At flank speed, the valiant little *Lupo* rushed back from the van, firing its small guns and making smoke in a vain attempt to hide its charges. The corvette was swiftly bracketed by enemy fire and limped off, fortunate to survive at all. The British searchlight crews fastened their fatal glare on boat after boat, each illumination followed by a burst of shells and bullets. Destroyers and cruisers rammed headlong into a number of caïques, slicing them in half, then churned through the men massed in the water. Bringing up the rear in a caïque designated S-8, a lieutenant named Hormann watched the British ships circle inshore to cut off any advance. He

saw a convoy vessel catch fire and disappear in a ball of flame as its munitions exploded. His turn came when a destroyer raced by, raking the S-8 with machine-gun bullets. The mainmast was shattered and crashed loudly to the deck. In a frenzy, two troopers cast off a life raft and jumped in—only to be riddled by enemy fire. The rest of the men flattened themselves on the deck in terror. Somehow, the S-8 remained afloat and drifted slowly out of the combat zone.

After two and a half hours, the shooting stopped and the searchlights were finally extinguished. At least a dozen caïques and three small freighters, all of them crammed with troops, had been sunk, and the pitiful survivors of the Maleme flotilla straggled northward toward Greece, returning their cargoes of dead and wounded. Britain's Admiral Cunningham estimated that 4,000 men had gone down with the ships. At German headquarters in Athens, Generals Kurt Student and Julius Ringel knew that the number of those embarked was little more than half that total, but they believed that virtually all had perished.

A miracle, however, was in the making. Most of the Germans had plunged overboard during the attacks. Gunfire and the thrashing propellers had killed some, but the great majority had escaped and their life jackets kept them afloat in the warm waters. In the morning, Italian boats and seaplanes mounted a massive rescue effort. And as the Ju 52s of the XI Air Corps resumed their airlift of mountain battalions into Maleme, the soldiers on board the planes dropped life rafts to their shipwrecked fellows below. By four in the afternoon on May 22, the rescue operation had almost been completed. Of the 2,331 troops on board the ill-fated flotilla, only about 300 were dead or missing. Nevertheless, it was clear that the units fighting at Maleme could not be relieved by sea—at least not immediately.

Any residual hope for swift seaborne reinforcement, even by day, had been extinguished earlier that morning when a second flotilla of thirty-eight small ships had departed Melos. They carried about 4,000 men, including the 2d Battalion of the 85th Mountain Regiment, and much-needed heavy weaponry. Originally, the flotilla had been scheduled to land at Heraklion, but now it was ordered to Maleme. The convoy had not gone far when, at about half past eight, a second Royal Navy task force spotted the first few caïques. Despite the certainty that Luftwaffe squadrons would soon be buzzing like hornets overhead, the four cruisers and three destroyers pressed on after their prey. As before, a lone Italian corvette, the *Sagittario*, gallantly made smoke and tried to draw the enemy's fire. By ten, the British were aware of the full extent of the convoy. Another duckshoot like the one off Maleme seemed in the making, as the troop-laden boats reversed course for home with little hope of escape.

On the morning following the repulse of the first invasion flotilla, Italian sailors transfer an oil-soaked German from their lifeboat to a rescue vessel. They had plucked the half-drowned soldier from the Sea of Crete.

In fact, they would escape, because Admiral Cunningham's commanders had tarried too long. On this morning in the waters off Crete, the Royal Navy would feel the sting of General Wolfram von Richthofen's VIII Air Corps. Dawn reconnaissance flights had reported dozens of British ships—not just the force approaching the troop convoy, but many others to the north and west. They were in range and without air cover.

From airfields across central Greece, the Peloponnesus, and the Aegean Islands, hundreds of fighters and bombers roared into the early-morning sky. Their pilots were determined not only to avenge yesterday's convoy fiasco, but to settle scores for the Luftwaffe's defeat in the recent Battle of Britain. At the airfield at Molaoi, Lieut. Colonel Oskar Dinort, commander of Stukageschwader 2, briefed his crews. Within minutes, scores of Ju 87s were in the air. Twenty-five miles north of Crete, the dive-bomber group found and attacked two British cruisers and a pair of destroyers.

The Stukas plummeted out of the morning sun, each releasing a single heavy bomb or four 110-pounders. Zigzagging at maximum speed, the British ships sought frantically to dodge the bombs while their gun crews sent up clouds of ack-ack. The sea boiled with near misses, and the ships steamed through mast-high geysers of water. Incredibly, all the heavy bombs missed; only a few light ones hit the superstructure of the cruisers *Gloucester* and *Fiji*. After ninety minutes, the flak-pocked Stukas peeled away to refuel and rearm, and the British ships retired westward.

To the east, meanwhile, the British force was about to pounce on the caïque convoy when help arrived in the form of a Ju 88 bomber *Gruppe*, or wing. Faster than the Ju 87 and able to carry a heavier payload, the twin-engine Ju 88 was beginning to earn a reputation as one of the war's most effective multipurpose planes. Minutes after taking off from a field near Athens, Captain Cuno Hoffmann and his *Gruppe* of Ju 88s looked down on a fascinating sight: The German "midget fleet," as they called it, was sailing northward in slow motion, the British were pursuing a few miles astern, and, between the two, the little Italian *Sagittario* dashed back and forth, laying a smoke screen and firing its puny guns.

The lead Ju 88s rolled in to attack—and met a wall of flak. The first bombs bracketed the cruiser *Naiad*. The ship slowed to half-speed but was still able to maneuver handily. More Ju 88s joined the fight, but the *Naiad* somehow evaded their bombs. By now, the British admiral had broken off pursuit of the convoy and was retreating westward in order to rendezvous with the main British fleet for joint protection. From Alexandria, Admiral Cunningham tried to countermand the move. He was convinced that destruction of the flotilla was worth almost any sacrifice, and that the warships would be safer from air attack among the German boats than on the open sea. "Stick to it!" he urged by radio. But his order arrived after the convoy had scattered and made its escape.

For three and a half hours, the battle raged on. High-flying Do 17s from Kampfgeschwader 2 and Me 109s from Jagdgeschwader 77 joined the Ju 88s. More near misses put two of the *Naiad*'s turrets out of action and ruptured the ship's hull plates. A Messerschmitt sprayed the bridge of the cruiser *Carlisle* with machine-gun fire, killing the captain. By early afternoon, the fleeing British ships had joined their main battle fleet in the Antikythera Strait, off the northwest coast of Crete. Now there were nineteen warships in all, led by the battleships *Warspite* and *Valiant*. But the bombs continued to fall, and within ten minutes, the *Warspite* suffered a direct hit. Me 109s attacking head-on soon took out the *Warspite*'s starboard four-inch and six-inch batteries. Casualties were mounting, but so far, in a day of furious air-sea battle, not a single British ship had been sunk.

The rearmed and refueled Stukas of Stukageschwader 2 then joined the attack. Aloft in his command aircraft, Colonel Dinort watched the British fleet—the two battleships, plus five cruisers and a dozen destroyers—change course to the south and then southwest. The enemy was leaving the arena. The Luftwaffe had driven the Royal Navy from the Sea of Crete.

Now Richthofen's fliers began to inflict fatal punishment. A pair of Stukas with heavy bombs scored direct hits on the destroyer *Greyhound* and sent it to the bottom. Two destroyers were diverted to pick up survivors. The

cruisers *Gloucester* and *Fiji* were to provide antiaircraft protection, but they had used up most of their ammunition and could put up only a feeble screen against the attacks. The *Gloucester* took at least five hits and burst into flames that embroiled its entire length. After a few minutes, massive internal explosions put the ship under. The *Fiji* broke away and raced for safety. It was almost out of range when a lone Me 109 streaked in and planted a 550-pound bomb alongside that buckled the ship's plates, causing a list and reducing its speed. The *Fiji* might still have escaped had not a second plane placed three 110-pound bombs over the cruiser's forward boiler room half an hour later. At dusk, the *Fiji* capsized and went down.

In his war diary, the exultant Richthofen wrote: "The British take hit after hit; ships burn and sink. Others turn aside to help and are caught by bombs, too. Some limp along with a list, others with a trail of oil, to get out of this hell. Flight units that have flown the whole day, bombed, reloaded with time for naught else, at evening begin to let out triumphant shouts of joy. Results cannot yet be assessed, but I have the solid feeling of a grand and decisive success: Six cruisers and three destroyers are definitely sunk, others so damaged they will sink in the night. We have finally demonstrated that, if weather permits flying, a fleet cannot operate within range of the Luftwaffe." Richthofen pressed for the immediate resumption of troop landings by sea "since these forces are urgently needed on Crete. The British ships, beaten and shot out, are retreating." But the destruction of the first Maleme flotilla had been too great a shock for the high command to recover from swiftly. Richthofen's suggestion was rejected; reinforcements would continue to go in by air.

Curiously, Hitler, too, failed to appreciate the Luftwaffe's triumph. The great news was immediately flashed to Reich Marshal Hermann Göring, who lost no time informing the Führer at his Berghof retreat. But there was only silence from Hitler—no orders, no messages of congratulation. Hitler seemed totally preoccupied with the forthcoming invasion of Russia.

The actual toll on the Royal Navy since the invasion had begun was considerable, though less than the Germans believed—two cruisers and two destroyers sunk, another three warships severely damaged, more than 1,000 men lost. And the engagement was not quite ended. The next morning, May 23, two dozen Stukas of Colonel Dinort's dive-bomber group discovered three destroyers that had remained behind overnight in order to shell German positions at Maleme. Ignoring meager antiaircraft fire, Dinort's dive bombers almost casually sank two of the destroyers, the *Kelly* and *Kashmir*, with direct hits. The third destroyer barely escaped after it had picked up 281 survivors.

The British had lost a perilously large portion of their Mediterranean

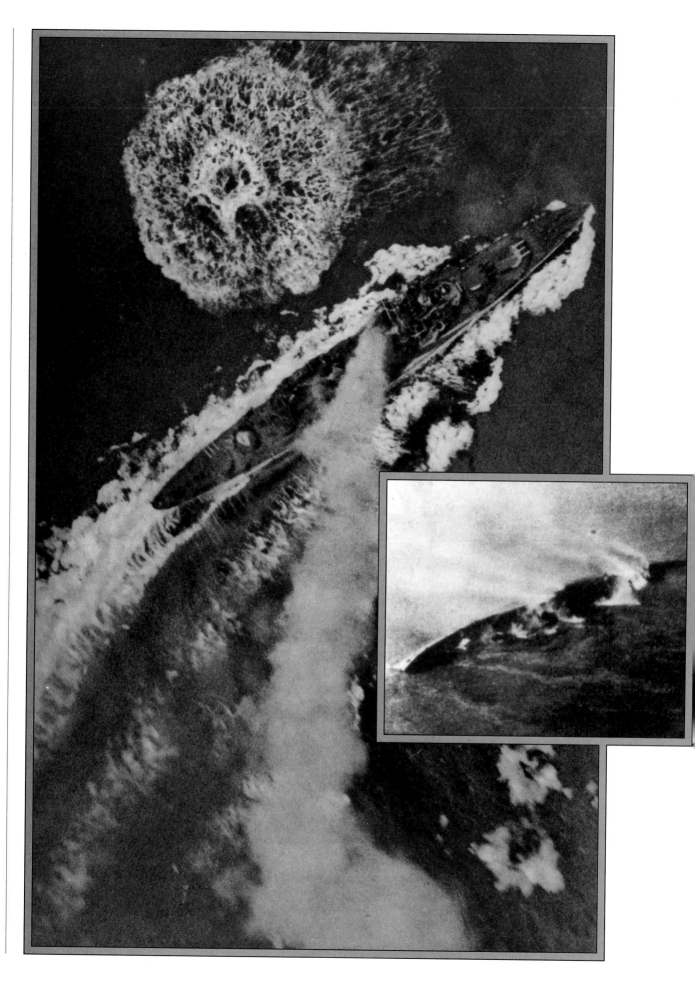

Fleet. Appraising the debacle, Admiral Cunningham signaled London: "The operations of the last four days have been nothing short of a test of strength between the Mediterranean Fleet and the German air force. I am afraid that, in the coastal area, we have to admit defeat and accept the fact that losses are too great to justify us in trying to prevent seaborne attacks on Crete. This is a melancholy conclusion, but it must be faced."

Yet on Crete itself, the battle was still balanced "on a knife edge," as General Ringel aptly put it. The British clearly held the upper hand at Galatas, Retimo, and Heraklion, while the Germans slowly tightened their grip on the all-important airfield at Maleme to the west.

In the eastern part of the island, the airborne invaders had been reduced to isolated pockets of men fighting furiously to save themselves from annihilation. Near Galatas on May 21, Colonel Richard Heidrich continued to deploy the weary paratroopers of his 3d Regiment in a series of bloody and fruitless attacks on the heights guarding the approaches to town. By evening, the enemy still held the high ground. Heidrich and his exhausted men remained bottled up in Prison Valley—and highly vulnerable to a counterattack that did not develop.

The remnants of Colonel Alfred Sturm's 2d Paratroop Regiment at Retimo—about 150 men under Major Hans Kroh on Hill A, near the landing strip, and Captain Oskar Wiedemann's two companies on the outskirts of town—tried to improve their positions during the morning on May 21. But Kroh's dawn assault on the landing strip ran into a vigorous counterattack by a company of Australian defenders. After reinforcements had added to their weight, the Australians drove the paratroopers northeastward off Hill A, toward the sea. Worse, Kroh watched in horror as a flight of Luftwaffe planes, unable to distinguish friend from foe, dived on his men, killing sixteen. In desperation, the paratroopers retreated to the grounds of a large olive-oil factory on the coast road and dug in for a last-ditch defense.

Wiedemann's paratroopers, at the roadblock east of Retimo, also came under heavy attack and were hemmed in by Cretan gendarmes and units of the Greek army. To make matters worse, the Australians had captured German plans and codes along with Colonel Sturm, and they used the codes to call in Luftwaffe strikes on Wiedemann's position. The only thing the paratroopers could do was cling to the ground they held and hope that reinforcements would somehow reach them.

At Heraklion on May 21, Colonel Bruno Bräuer's dawn attack on the airfield had ended in disaster. His troops were stopped by concentrated fire from the Black Watch Battalion posted there, then driven by determined Cretan irregulars into a defensive perimeter on a ridge two miles

The British heavy cruiser *Gloucester* turns to starboard and narrowly dodges a Luftwaffe bomb during a running air-sea battle northwest of Crete on May 22. Later, after several direct hits, the *Gloucester* heeled irretrievably to port *(inset)* and sank with great loss of life.

southeast of the field. A German platoon penetrated the high ground east of the field, but it was quickly isolated and overrun, its lieutenant slain.

Meanwhile, the detachment under Major Karl-Lothar Schulz that had reached Heraklion harbor during the first night tried all the next day to drive through the town and on to the airfield. At midafternoon, Heraklion's defenders were near surrender when the arrival of two platoons of British regulars encouraged them to continue fighting. At dusk on May 21, the 400 survivors of Schulz's force had to retreat to their starting point, west of the city. Before the next day's fighting ended, the British and their allies would count more than 1,200 dead Germans on the battlefield.

In effect, Heraklion then became a sideshow—like Retimo. German headquarters in Athens put an encouraging face on the twin predicaments by reporting that the besieged troopers were "tying down enemy forces and preventing use of the airfields by the RAF." In fact, Athens had ordered the paratroopers to hang on as best they could until the fight for Maleme had ended in victory and the forces there could break out to the east.

At Maleme early on May 22, Colonel Ramcke and his men watched in dismay as the blue-white shafts of searchlight beams and the bright orange beacons of burning ships illuminated the seaward horizon. They knew immediately what the distant light show signified—the destruction of the caïque flotilla. They could expect no reinforcement the next day, except by air. Now was the time for the British to counterattack in force.

Attack was precisely what the Allied commander, General Sir Bernard Freyberg, had in mind. From the moment he learned of the loss of Hill 107 and the airfield, he had known that a powerful counterattack was critical. He assigned the mission to Brigadier Edward Puttick of the New Zealand Division, who turned it over to Brigadier James Hargest of the 5th New Zealand Brigade, who detailed two of his five battalions to launch the assault. All three commanders were afraid of things that had not yet happened. Freyberg feared more paratroop landings and still expected an invasion by sea, despite clear evidence of the convoy's defeat. He thus contemplated attack from every direction at any minute and felt compelled to husband his forces.

Puttick shared this state of mind. Intent on guarding his rear and the beach, he was unwilling to risk much to regain the airfield. Hargest took this defensive attitude a step further, recommending against attacking in daylight under the guns and bombs of the Luftwaffe, even though it had been demonstrated that the closer troops came to the enemy, the safer they were from enemy planes. Hargest spent much of the night moving units around to make sure the beaches and his headquarters were secure against

A Relentless Push to the East

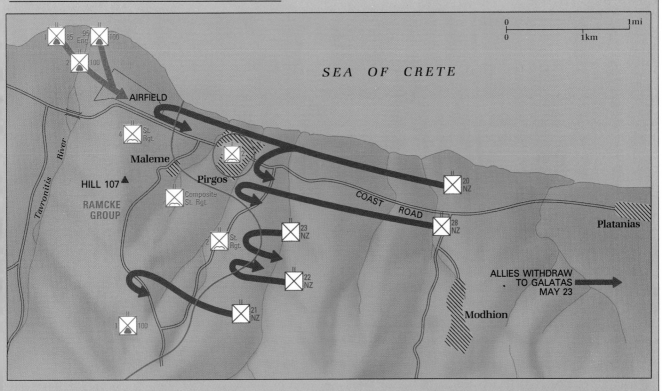

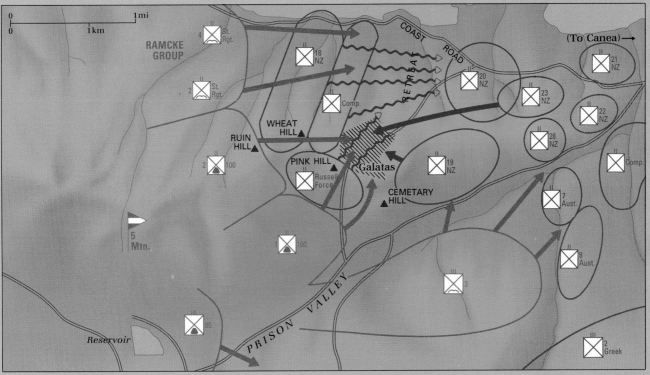

The arrival of a battalion of the 100th Mountain Regiment in the afternoon on May 21 strengthened the paratroopers' toehold at Maleme *(top)*. That night, the Germans turned back a counterattack by New Zealanders trying to recapture Hill 107 and the airstrip. The next day, three more battalions of mountain troops landed. As the defenders fell back on Galatas, Colonel Bernhard Ramcke formed the surviving paratroopers into one group for an advance eastward along the coast. The mountain troops on their right pursued the retreating Allies across the rugged interior. The bottom map shows the Germans' attack. In the afternoon on May 25, they drove in the enemy center at Galatas, ending the Allies' last hope of holding the island.

a landing from the sea. In consequence, his counterattack was late, hesitant, and woefully weak.

Only two hours of darkness remained when the New Zealand infantry, supported by three light tanks, at last moved out toward the village of Pirgos, three miles away. From there, the 20th New Zealand Battalion had orders to drive straight ahead to the airfield while the 28th Battalion veered left to attack Hill 107.

Almost immediately, the New Zealanders ran into pockets of paratroopers who had taken cover in houses, gardens, and fields along their route. Nasty firefights erupted along the line, and both sides took heavy casualties. The Germans were caught by surprise, but resistance stiffened as the New Zealanders encountered the main body of Ramcke's replenished Sturmregiment. Dawn found the attackers fighting hand to hand through Pirgos, still a mile short of both the airfield and Hill 107.

By this time, the Luftwaffe was aloft in force, strafing and bombing at will. The New Zealanders' tanks were destroyed or driven to cover, and the infantrymen hunkered down in fear as German planes wove back and forth above the treetops. Soon the airlift of mountain troops resumed for the day, and a steady flow of Ju 52s began landing at Maleme. Forward elements of the New Zealanders could see the field and watched the mountaineers, as one officer recalled, "jumping out and getting straight into battle."

The tide of combat carried the remnants of one company of the 20th New Zealand to the edge of the airfield, where they fired a few shots into the stream of Ju 52s setting down, unloading, and taking off again. It was broad daylight, reported the company commander, and "we had come under the most intense mortar and machine-gun fire with the clear ground of the aerodrome in front of us. I pulled the company back about 100 yards into the cover of some bamboos." That, as it turned out, was the high-water mark of the counterattack. Ignoring the pleas for reinforcements from his battalion commanders, the ever-preoccupied Brigadier Hargest refused to commit his full strength to battle, and by midafternoon, the New Zealanders had begun pulling back. The counterattack had failed.

That day at Maleme, Ju 52s of the XI Air Corps landed three more battalions of mountain troops and a field hospital, along with heavy weapons, artillery, and ammunition. It was a chaotic and extremely dangerous operation, because the airfield was still under artillery fire from the east. The big, trimotor Junkers were coming down in flocks, and a dust cloud billowed over the field. The transports disappeared into the miasma, their cargo of infantrymen piled out, and the planes rose again. One of the mountain troops recalled that as he and his comrades leaped from the aircraft, "the wind of the propellers blew the yellow dust in our faces. The

Captured members of the 2d Paratroop Regiment, some of them with bandaged wounds, line a street in Retimo on May 21. An Australian officer praised the gritty Germans as a "gallant and chivalrous foe."

Junkers was already moving again. A shell burst very close. The crash of the burst, the noise of the engines, the dust, and the shouting of the ground crews made our heads swim."

The soldiers tumbled into a nearby bomb crater to get their bearings. "Our Junkers was hardly away when the next one landed right in the middle of the thick dust. A cracking, rending sound. More clouds of dust. Crash! A belly landing. The undercarriage flies in huge bounds into the nearby water." As before, captured Bren carriers dragged the wrecked aircraft to the side, and the landings continued. The losses, in the words of the XI Air Corps's report, were "within acceptable limits."

Early in the day, General Student realized that he had been correct in

gambling everything on Maleme, and he prepared to move his headquarters there to assume command on Crete. His confidence was reinforced by the failure of the British counterattack, by the throng of transports landing safely, and by an erroneous report from his chief of staff that the Maleme flotilla had made it through after all.

Generals Wolfram von Richthofen and Alexander Löhr, however, were increasingly edgy about the confused situation on the island. In their view, the man to sort things out was the 5th Mountain Division's judicious General Ringel. They thought it vital that Student and the staff of his XI Air Corps remain in Greece in order to oversee the flow of men and supplies to Crete. After a day-long wrangle and an appeal to the high command, Student was ordered to stay in Athens. Everything remaining of the 5th Mountain Division—including those troops returned from the second caïque flotilla—and the 141st Regiment of the 6th Mountain Division would be dispatched to Maleme. According to the VIII Air Corps's diary, "The impression now is that things will get cracking with the necessary energy, clarity, and decisiveness."

Fresh mountain troops disembark from their transport at the airfield at Maleme, ready for combat. They were among the three battalions flown in on May 22 to strengthen the Germans' shaky grip on Hill 107, which rises in the background.

Ringel's orders, hand-delivered by General Löhr, were to secure the airfield, clear the Suda Bay area, relieve the paratroopers in Prison Valley, drive to Retimo and Heraklion, and then mop up Crete. Löhr leaned forward emotionally. "*Servus*, Ringel!" he said. "Farewell. Make it good!" Ringel and his staff took off at five o'clock that evening in five Ju 52s. An equal number of Me 109s escorted them. There was a moment of excitement at Maleme when Ringel's plane belly-landed on the beach because the field itself was under fire, but everyone got down safely. By dark, the general had sized up the situation and restructured the invasion force.

Ringel ordered Colonel Ramcke, who had been dashing between units on the backseat of a motorcycle, to organize all surviving paratroopers at Maleme into one combat group and lead them eastward in a drive along the coast road. On Ramcke's right, Colonel Willibald Utz and two battalions of the 100th Mountain Regiment would continue a flanking movement along a front stretching inland across the hilly country southeast of the airfield. A third mountain battalion from the 85th Regiment, under Colonel August Krakau, would swing farther south in a deep envelopment designed to take out enemy artillery positions. With an engineer battalion deployed to protect the airfield perimeter from the west and south, Ringel's preparations were complete. He was ready to drive toward Galatas, Canea, and Suda Bay at dawn on May 23.

Confusion beset the New Zealanders facing Ringel. Watching the heavy air traffic at Maleme, the 5th Brigade's Hargest at first deluded himself into thinking that his halfhearted counterattack had succeeded and that the Germans were evacuating by air. When he was disabused of that notion,

he persisted in a rosy estimate of the situation. "Officers on the ground believe enemy preparing for attack and take a serious view," he informed General Freyberg. "I disagree, but, of course, they have a closer view." He gave more credence to another report, equally distant from his headquarters, of renewed German activity in Prison Valley. Thus Hargest did nothing about his front lines but asked Freyberg to protect his rear. Instead, Freyberg planned a renewal at dawn of the failed attack on the airfield at Maleme, this time with two brigades instead of two battalions. But his resolve lasted only until he heard gunfire in the east, coming from behind him. That part of Hargest's report had been right enough; German paratroopers in Prison Valley were on the move.

Despite the earlier setbacks, the 3d Paratroop Regiment's Colonel Heidrich was nothing if not aggressive, and he found his stalemated position in the valley intolerably galling. His men were frustrated and hungry, their morale slipping. Far better to do something than nothing, he thought. Late on May 21, Heidrich ordered the remnants of his 2d Battalion, under Major Helmut Derpa, to renew the assault against the heights around Galatas. When Derpa expressed doubts about the attack, Heidrich exploded and accused him of cowardice. Derpa grew furious; no one could say that to a German paratroop major. And the following day, he led his men forward.

Derpa's battalion carved out a toehold on the heights, then became enmeshed in a brutal firefight. From the direction of Galatas came a wild and incredible charge by 100 screaming, shooting Greeks and Cretan villagers led by a lone British officer. The sight and sound of the charge unnerved the tired Germans, who retreated from their hard-won positions. Major Derpa came off the hills on a stretcher and died of wounds soon after.

Heidrich's second attack started as no more than a probe, but it produced unexpectedly large dividends. While his comrades were hung up along the Galatas road, Major Ludwig Heilmann and 141 men and nine officers worked west, hoping to swing around and cut the coast road. Moving cautiously, Heilmann was still a mile short of the road as the sun rose on May 23. For the moment, all that he could achieve was a series of vigorous skirmishes with Allied units, but the sound of his chattering machine guns and exaggerated reports of heavy fighting had a stunning effect on the Allied command.

Freyberg was about to order an all-out assault on the Maleme airfield. But now that he apparently faced an attack from the rear, he paused and conferred with his subordinates. The divisional commander, Brigadier Puttick, voiced fears of being cut off and recommended withdrawal. The 5th Brigade's Hargest pronounced his men too tired to attack in any case, and that sealed the decision. Instead of striking out vigorously, Freyberg agreed to retreat from Maleme and consolidate his forces around Galatas. The move strengthened Allied positions in preparation for the expected German advance but, as Freyberg's chief of staff later commented, "amounted to accepting the loss of Crete."

Surprised by the lack of resistance, Ringel's steadily growing force pushed eastward along the coast road and through the inland foothills. The New Zealanders, who had been determined to attack again, fell back resentfully. Ramcke recommended "plunging on after the broken defenders," and from Athens, Student urged haste to relieve the trapped paratroopers at Retimo and Heraklion. Ringel, however, insisted on a deliberate, carefully orchestrated pace. One of the general's favorite mottoes was "Sweat saves blood," and he remained true to it now.

Although the going was relatively easy along the coast, the mountain troops on the southern flank were having a bad time of it as they struggled across the dry, sharp-edged terrain. "My troops crawled over land that the devil created in anger," wrote Ringel later. "Man by man, overloaded, gasping, bathed in sweat." The Greeks and Cretan irregulars harried them incessantly, and there were reports of atrocities, of German wounded being hideously tortured, of the dead being mutilated and robbed. The 5th Division reacted by declaring that ten Cretans were to be shot in reprisal for each paratrooper killed in that fashion. Houses and farms from which attacks on Germans had originated were to be destroyed, and hostages were to be taken from every offending village and town. For a civilian to be found armed was tantamount to a death sentence.

Feelings among the Germans grew stronger still when the first units of Ramcke's Sturmregiment moved from Pirgos to where the regiment's 3d Battalion had been slaughtered on the first day. Captain Walter Gericke, a hardened trooper whose 4th Battalion had been in the thick of it from the start, was not prepared for what he saw. "Among the boughs of the olive trees could be seen the white silk of the parachutes, with their tangles of twisted cords," he wrote. "Dead parachutists hung suspended from the branches, swinging gently to and fro on the light breeze. Those who had succeeded in getting free had been shot down within a few strides or slain by Cretan volunteers. The pockets of their uniforms had been torn open. Equipment lay strewn in all directions—grenades, helmets, weapons, a bayonet stuck in the sand, ammunition boxes, packets of bandages, a water container filled with stinking water, postcards, photographs. Here and there lay a dead Englishman or New Zealander. All alike had turned black in the blazing heat. Around them buzzed the fat, blue flies."

Gericke and his men pushed grimly on. But after a day of relatively easy

Atrocities in the Olive Groves

Of the many ugly surprises that Crete provided, none staggered the Germans more than the belligerence of the Cretans themselves. Instead of submissive civilians, the invaders encountered stubborn and courageous foes, ready to defend their island home—as they had for hundreds of years—with whatever weapons came to hand: hunting rifles, aged pistols, axes, pitchforks, scissors, even rocks.

Men, women, and children fell upon the Germans with a fury, asking no quarter and giving none. "Old men fought like youths, and young boys fought like men," said a German officer. "They have no right to fight us; they're civilians!"

For the advancing paratroopers, danger lurked down every village path and behind every tree. Those who fell into Cretan hands could expect a brutal death. The Germans found the bodies of scores of their comrades with throats slit, eyes gouged out, chests ripped open, noses, ears, and genitals cut off. Infuriated, the Germans retaliated with draconian tactics of their own. The Luftwaffe dropped leaflets whose chilling message would soon become familiar throughout Europe: Ten Cretans would be shot for every soldier killed by civilians.

The Germans took hostages, burned farms, and firebombed an entire village (above, near right), but the Cretans only fought harder. Many of them fled to the mountains and continued the struggle until 1945, when the last of the Germans abandoned the island.

A German soldier (*left*) studies a newly erected sign, written in German and Greek, declaring that the village of Kandanos had been destroyed "in retribution for the bestial murder of a paratroop platoon and half of an engineer platoon by armed men and women in ambush."

In a quiet olive grove (*right*) paratroopers take aim at Cretan civilians. In their effort to crush all resistance, the vengeful Germans siezed males between the ages of eighteen and fifty-five and shot many of them in retaliation for attacks on Germans.

Cretan civilians *(below)* fall in a hail of bullets from a German firing squad. In 1946, General Kurt Student, the officer who ordered the mass executions, was convicted of war crimes by a British military court and sentenced to five years in prison. The verdict was later overturned; the reprisals were held to be justifiable wartime measures.

progress on May 23, Ringel ordered a temporary halt on the coast road while the forces inland continued their flanking movement. Late that evening, elements of the 100th Mountain Regiment made contact with the remnants of Heidrich's 3d Paratroop Regiment in Prison Valley. Colonel Utz climbed into a motorcycle sidecar and drove to meet Heidrich and his thirsty, hungry, hollow-eyed troopers in the hamlet of Mandhara, on the west slope of the valley. Heidrich, in a show of casualness, offered Utz a cigar. Then, in a choking voice, he said, "Good, you've come!"

Faithful to his design, Ringel continued to move slowly forward on May

The course of battle running with them at last, Colonel Ramcke's paratroopers stand guard over captured New Zealanders huddled beneath an ancient stone wall. The bodies at right are New Zealand dead.

24, taking time to bring up artillery, heavy weapons, and more reinforcements from Maleme. On the coast road, Ramcke's troopers linked up—amid much backslapping—with Heilmann's detachment of skirmishers. To Ramcke's right, the 100th Mountain Regiment edged into position facing the main Allied defenses in the hills south and west of Galatas. Despite their ordeal—or possibly because of it—Heidrich's weary paratroopers were determined to stay in the fight. From their position on the right in Prison Valley, they poised to drive northeast, toward the coast. Ringel placed the two battalions of the 85th Mountain Regiment opposite Alikianou, ready to strike across the Allies' rear and prevent their flight.

Not until the night of May 24 was Ringel satisfied with the placement of his little army. It now numbered more than 4,000 troops, at least half of them fresh and superbly armed mountaineers. Behind them, another regiment had landed and was moving up to take its place in the line. The soldiers were buoyed as well, not only by what they could observe around them, but by Berlin's acknowledgment, at last, of their existence. Since the first calamitous hours of the invasion, the Wehrmacht's official communiqués had avoided any reference to land fighting on Crete. The pointed omission had only increased the misgivings of the desperately fighting men. But on the evening of May 24, German radio broadcast with great fanfare a special announcement: Airborne troops had been in action on Crete for five days, important positions had been won, and the western end of the island was already in German hands.

The attackers relaxed. As the war diary of the 6th Mountain Division dryly put it, "The situation appeared to be sufficiently under control to allow information on the fighting to be issued from now on." In a wink, even the hard-pressed paratroopers at Retimo and Heraklion recovered their élan, and they audaciously demanded the surrender of their besiegers.

In truth, the Allies had been backed into a dangerously constricted position; the Germans were well around their left flank. The defenders temporarily enjoyed an edge in numbers, but only 1,800 men were on the Galatas line, where the German attack must surely come. Nearby, 1,600 were in reserve, 1,065 Australians were posted along the Prison Valley Road toward Canea, and 2,000 fresh troops were preparing to defend Canea itself.

The defenders lacked food and ammunition—and more than that, their confidence was gone. The Luftwaffe had literally wrung it from them. Never before had such a vast armada of close-support aircraft operated at will above an exposed and defenseless enemy. At Dunkirk, the defeated divisions had found their salvation not only in the Royal Navy, but in the RAF, which flew protective cover overhead. In the battle for Crete, there was nothing to oppose the Luftwaffe. Weeks of unremitting air attack in advance

of the invasion had taken a heavy toll, psychological as well as physical. Because the German planes bombed and strafed from dawn to dusk, the Allies could accomplish nothing significant by day; all resupply had to be done at night. For the men burrowing into the earth and sheltering behind walls, the continuous noise and concussion became almost unbearable, and helpless lethargy afflicted many of them. Even the unquestionably brave Brigadier Hargest confessed that the air attacks on Crete induced in him a "kind of dread."

On the morning of May 25, General Student flew into Maleme and immediately motored east to visit his cherished paratroopers. He knew most of them by name and was stunned at how many had perished. Student then went to the headquarters of the 5th Mountain Division to take command of the final drive. The timing of his arrival embarrassed Ringel. Having so carefully prepared the stage for the decisive attack, he wanted it well under way by the time Student arrived. It was almost five in the evening, after a day of spasmodic artillery and air bombardment, when the German infantry rose from cover and surged forward. At that same moment, flights of deadly Stukas appeared overhead.

The entrenched Allies fought back savagely. "These hammer blows seem to affect the New Zealanders like mineral baths," recalled a German soldier. "Frantic, hellish fire keeps raking us whenever we raise our heads." But the weight of the attack was irresistible. Ramcke's troops pressed eastward

Entering Galatas on May 26, victorious German troops pass an abandoned tank and a dead Allied soldier. The light tank was one of two the town's New Zealand defenders had used against the invaders the night before.

Exhausted mountain troops pause to nurse their wounds after the bitter fight for Galatas. Thrown out of the town by a fierce Allied counterattack, the Germans spent a chilly night without food, water, or blankets.

along the coast road for a mile, then held up, under orders not to move too far ahead of the others.

To their south, Utz's 2d Battalion, under Major Otto Schury, stormed through heavy fire down a slope called Ruin Hill, then up another named Wheat Hill. From there, the men looked down into the heart of Galatas. To their right, Utz's 1st Battalion, led by Major Max-Günther Schrank, clawed up Pink Hill and Cemetery Hill, where Heidrich had been repulsed on the first day. Now the Germans outgunned their opponents, and by nightfall, elements of the two battalions had forced their way into Galatas.

The fighting had only begun. As the mountaineers pushed up the narrow streets toward the center of town, they collided head-on with counterattacking New Zealanders led by a pair of tanks. The warning cry *"Panzer!"* rang out, and the Germans let go with every weapon they had with them. "Firing out of all barrels, one tank rolls up within twenty meters," noted a German sergeant. "We are blinded as well as deafened. The riflemen shoot what they can. We throw grenade after grenade. Finally, a track breaks, but the tank keeps shooting."

On the balcony of a nearby house, two machine gunners hammered away at the enemy armor. "A comrade runs down the stairs and lays a balled charge under the tank's belly," wrote a mountain trooper. "Down we go into the street. Suddenly, we are faced by several Tommies with lowered bayonets. Lightning fast, our lieutenant whips out his machine pistol and empties a magazine into the attackers." The lieutenant was immediately slain, and the fight became a melee. Amid sudden bursts of firing and grenade explosions and screams and curses, groups of men met in the darkened alleys. The struggle was particularly bitter around the church in the town square. There, knots of Germans loosed torrents of fire at foes they could not see, aiming for the muzzle flashes from their guns.

The fight continued into the night, until the New Zealanders mounted a thrust strong enough to drive the mountain troops from Galatas. The Germans retreated across slopes dotted with the bodies of those killed in the initial attack. Colonel Utz rallied them at Pink Hill, and the battle gradually dwindled to random shooting.

New Zealand officers on the scene knew that their victory would achieve nothing unless they could resume the attack. But that was not to be. As they conferred, a staff officer arrived from headquarters to veto any further advance. The divisional commander, Brigadier Puttick, either did not know or could not see the opportunity offered by the retaking of Galatas. "Heavy attacks about 2000 hours have obviously broken our line," he reported to General Freyberg. "Enemy is through at Galatas. Am exceedingly doubtful on present reports whether I can hold enemy tomorrow."

Freyberg advised him to maintain his new line in front of Canea at all costs. At the same time, he began planning to evacuate by sea from the island's south coast. Crete, he believed, was lost. The problem now was how to save his troops.

Hours of confusion followed as Freyberg moved his headquarters, dithered over chain-of-command questions, and pondered how to secure permission from Middle East Command for what had to be done. Puttick withdrew his intensely disappointed men not only from Galatas but to a second line east of Canea, taking up a more compact position before the village of Suda. The new line extended about a mile southward from the coast road at the point of Suda Bay. Puttick left only Force Reserve, a rear guard of 1,200 soldiers, to make a stand before Canea.

"The limit of endurance has been reached by troops under my command," Freyberg told Middle East headquarters in Cairo at half past eight in the morning. "Our position here is hopeless. The difficulties of extricating this force in full are now insuperable." If permission to evacuate were given immediately, he said, he might be able to save a "certain proportion." He received no immediate response.

In Galatas after the New Zealand retreat, the remainder of the night had passed in an eerie silence broken only by the murmurs and moans of the wounded combatants. A young Cretan girl, perhaps twelve years old, crept from the rubble and approached the twisted forms lying on the street before her. She covered some of them with carpets and pieces of cloth and, when she found life, returned with drinks of sweet goat's milk. Then she disappeared again into the ruins.

The first German patrols moving forward at dawn on May 26 were astonished to find the town of Galatas empty. There was no trace of the enemy, except for the wounded, the unburied dead, and discarded equipment. The patrols probed eastward after the New Zealanders but did not pursue them. Ringel was intent on shifting reinforcements to his right wing so they could lead the advance, curve northward to cut off the enemy's retreat, and trap its main force.

While Ringel built up his right, he asked the Luftwaffe to pound the Allied positions until four o'clock that afternoon, when he planned a general assault. His plan was derailed, however, when Luftwaffe pilots ranged too far south and attacked Colonel Krakau's 85th Regiment as it emerged from

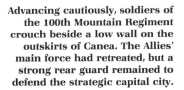

Advancing cautiously, soldiers of the 100th Mountain Regiment crouch beside a low wall on the outskirts of Canea. The Allies' main force had retreated, but a strong rear guard remained to defend the strategic capital city.

the hills after a harrowing fifty-mile march through the punishing Cretan terrain. Ringel screamed for the head of the offending flight leader, but the deed had been done. In the resulting confusion, only part of the line moved forward: the ever-combative Heidrich, leading the 3d Regiment paratroopers who had been bottled up for so long in Prison Valley. Accompanied by the newly arrived 141st Regiment of the 6th Mountain Division, Heidrich's troops swept easily to the edge of the plain of Canea.

"Absolute calm prevailed," reported the commander of Heidrich's 1st Battalion, Captain Friedrich-August von der Heydte. But Heidrich had orders not to enter Canea. Instead, his regiment and the 141st, under Colonel Maximilian Jais, were to continue the eastward enveloping movement, driving across the British line of retreat past Suda and onto the Akrotiri Peninsula. Ramcke's coastal group and Utz's 100th Mountain Regiment would seize Canea. Accordingly, Captain Heydte bedded down his troopers for the night, grumbling that "others would reap the glory" while he and his regiment did the dirty work of mopping up.

As it turned out, some very dirty work was needed the next morning—not involving the paratroopers but Jais and his 141st Mountain Regiment. Driving east toward Suda, Jais's 1st Battalion, led by Major Hans Forster, ran headlong into a dense enemy position a mile west of Suda. Although the bulk of the Allied forces had retreated eastward, parts of seven Australian and New Zealand battalions had dug in on a line scarcely 2,000 yards long. As the Germans approached, the Allied position erupted in flame. A screaming Anzac bayonet charge followed, and within a few minutes, 300 of Forster's men were killed or wounded, the rest put to rout. But as before, the Allies could not hold what they had won. They returned to their original line, having gained only time for the main Allied force to retreat southward.

In the interim, Heidrich's 1st Battalion, under Captain Heydte, had reached the neck of the Akrotiri Peninsula, halfway between Canea and Suda. There, Heydte paused, uncertain of what to do. The sounds of fighting from the west soon convinced him that to push northward onto the peninsula would be folly. Instead, he led his battalion west, into Canea. The glory of seizing the capital of Crete would be his after all.

"It proved a march, not a combat advance," reported Heydte. To warn away the Luftwaffe, his paratroopers went in holding swastika flags parallel to the ground. Near the central plaza, the paratroopers came upon a hospital, and wounded Germans poured from its doors, shouting for joy. Heydte set up his headquarters in the plaza. A lieutenant soon arrived with the mayor of Canea. Elegantly garbed—in contrast to the tattered German captain—the mayor explained that he wished to surrender the city and asked for "clemency." The young paratroop officer solemnly vouched for

On May 27, Colonel Ramcke's group and the 100th Mountain Regiment, advancing on Canea after its victory at Galatas, slammed into Force Reserve, a unit of 1,200 soldiers left behind to cover the Allied retreat. When the paratroopers and mountain troops overran this pugnacious rear guard, the 3d Paratroop Regiment swept into Canea. Meanwhile, the 141st and 85th Mountain Regiments, harassed by Cretans and Greek regulars, marched eastward to block the southward flight of the main Allied force. At "42d Street," a sunken dirt track running south from Suda Bay, a counterattack repulsed the 141st, enabling the Allies to elude the Germans.

Until the end of the campaign on June 1, German efforts focused largely on rescuing the trapped paratroopers at Retimo and Heraklion. The relief mission was assigned to Lieut. Colonel August Wittmann, who set out along the coast road with a hastily assembled flying column. The Allies, after a brush with lead elements of Wittmann's group southeast of Suda, pressed across the White Mountains to Sphakia, a fishing village on the southern coast, where the Royal Navy stood by to evacuate most of them. British destroyers also saved the garrison at Heraklion, but the troops at Retimo had to be abandoned to the Germans.

A Narrow Escape for the Allies

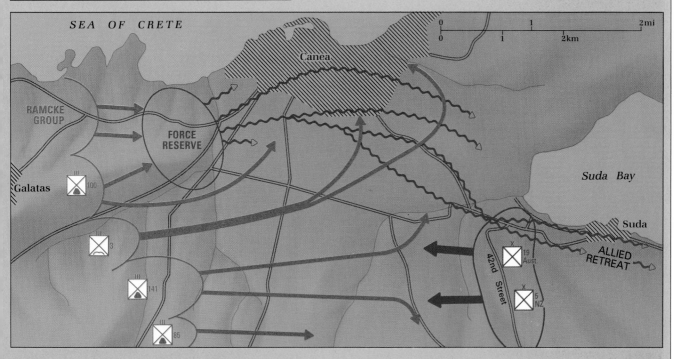

SEA OF CRETE

Canea

RAMCKE GROUP

FORCE RESERVE

Galatas

100

141

85

Suda Bay

Suda

19 Aust.

42nd Street

5 NZ

ALLIED RETREAT

0   1   2mi
0   1   2km

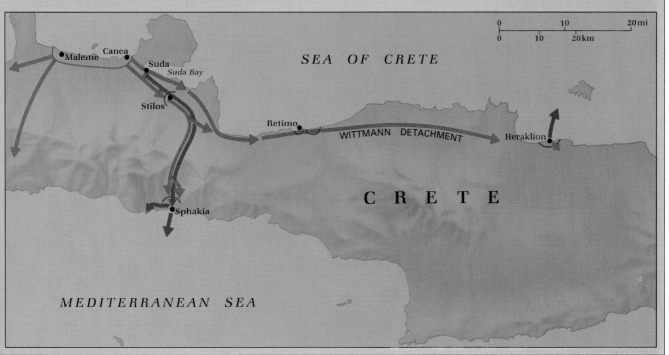

Maleme   Canea

Suda

Suda Bay

Stilos

SEA OF CRETE

Retimo

WITTMANN DETACHMENT

Heraklion

C R E T E

Sphakia

MEDITERRANEAN SEA

0   10   20mi
0   10   20km

his troops' behavior and sealed the surrender with a toast "to peace among men." Someone had found wine, and they drank from tin cups. Emerging into the sunlight, Heydte could see the German flag hoisted on a tall minaret overlooking the plaza.

Earlier that morning, May 27, Ramcke and Utz had launched their assault against Force Reserve, the unit standing between them and Canea. The Allies resisted sharply, but the rattle of German machine guns gradually extinguished the sound of Allied fire. Of the 1,200 soldiers in the rear guard, only 400 made it past the encircling Germans and joined their comrades in retreat, south of Suda. At three that afternoon, Ramcke's paratroopers and Utz's mountaineers swept into Canea—to find Heydte's men at ease, swimming happily in the coastal waters and staking out choice quarters in the seaside villas. As Heydte's adjutant remarked: "The battle for Canea is over. The fight for comfortable billets has now begun."

When the news was flashed to Athens, the German command was jubilant. "Bravo, Ringel!" radioed Field Marshal Wilhelm List, the commander in chief of German forces in Southeast Europe. "Appreciation and

Relieved after being cut off at Retimo for ten days, grim-faced paratroopers greet their commander in chief, General Kurt Student. Of roughly 1,500 men in their assault group, all but about 200 had been killed, wounded, or captured.

best wishes to the mountain troops." But it was a little early for such congratulations. A few miles east of Canea, the Allied line in front of Suda held firm, causing the German right wing to lapse into apprehensive immobility, and winning still more time for the British and Commonwealth forces to escape. Ringel's entrapment had failed.

Late in the evening before Canea fell, Freyberg had ordered a general withdrawal through the mountains to Sphakia, on the south coast. He acted despite suggestions to the contrary from Middle East Command, who, in response to his appeal for permission, advised that he retreat to Retimo. A cable from Churchill followed. "Victory in Crete essential at this turning point of the war," he wrote. "Keep hurling in all you can." Freyberg tried once more to introduce reality into the deliberations. He replied bluntly, "There is no possibility of hurling in reinforcements." In the afternoon, he finally gained approval for what he was already doing.

The Allied retreat begun that night was anything but orderly. "In the main, it was a disorganized rabble," Freyberg was to describe later. "Never shall I forget the almost complete lack of control of the masses on the move, that endless stream of trudging men." Sensing only that salvation lay in Sphakia, thousands of disheartened troops "doggedly and painfully" made their way to the fishing village.

As late as the morning of May 28, Ringel did not realize the Allies were running. He assumed that they were falling back along the coast road toward Retimo. Ringel was operating without his customary air arm; on May 26, the bulk of the Luftwaffe had been withdrawn to prepare for the invasion of the Soviet Union. Enough aerial reconnaissance remained for pilots to report that there was no sign of the British to the east, but Ringel shrugged off the information.

The mountain general was under great pressure. His superior, General Student, agonized over the fate of the paratroopers at Retimo and Heraklion, who by now had been trapped for a week. In order to relieve the two regiments, Ringel organized a flying column under his artillery commander, Lieut. Colonel August Wittmann. The rescue force included virtually every mobile unit the Germans had on Crete. Setting out along the coast road in the morning on May 28, Wittmann's men encountered a rear guard of commandos and New Zealand Maoris, who held them up for six hours before being driven off.

The column reached the town of Retimo early on May 30, and Student himself followed close behind. The Allied defenders, short of almost all supplies and unaware of the evacuation order, laid down their arms. In ten days of battle, they had inflicted terrible losses on the 2d Paratroop Reg-

Each paratrooper took to Crete a gravity knife that could be opened with one hand: At a flick of the lever, the blade dropped down from the handle. The sergeant who owned this knife carved the German name for the place where he fought—*Rethymnon*, or Retimo—on the grip.

iment: 700 dead and wounded, 500 captured. Barely 200 Germans were still fit to fight when relief arrived.

Meanwhile, the issue at Heraklion had also been decided. Royal Navy destroyers had evacuated the Allied garrison of 4,200 men during the night of May 28-29, greatly surprising and relieving the Germans trapped there. The next morning, however, some remaining Stukas found the ships and destroyed two of them, inflicting another 800 casualties.

The German drive to rescue the paratroopers at Retimo had been the deliverance of Freyberg's fleeing army. Only scattered patrols of Colonel Krakau's 85th Mountain Regiment had tried to follow the Allies into the southern mountains, and those patrols met a fiercely determined Greek

rear guard. Not until May 28 did elements of the mountain regiment's 2d Battalion reach the village of Stilos, where the road turned south toward Sphakia. When captured enemy officers revealed that the main body of Allied troops had passed through Stilos the day before, Ringel at last realized what Freyberg was doing. Even then, Ringel did not react with any urgency; he was convinced that the Allies could not escape from the island in any case. He contented himself with detaching two battalions of the 100th Mountain Regiment in belated pursuit.

By this time, the foremost units of the retreating army had already reached Sphakia, and that night four destroyers evacuated the first 1,100 soldiers. Throughout the next day, the German pursuers were delayed by a combination of the hard terrain, the rearguard action, and Colonel Utz's reluctance to bloody his men further in direct assaults. The cautious colonel favored flanking moves instead, and while they developed, the Royal Navy took another 6,000 troops off the island.

On May 30, German patrols moved down the ravines to the beach but were driven back. Out of radio contact with his superiors, Utz sent a messenger on a seven-hour-long drive to request air support from the Stukas that were still available. Then he mounted another flanking movement. By the last day of May, however, neither flanking force had reached the cliffs overlooking the beach, and only a few planes had turned up to harass the enemy from above.

The Allies used their two nights of grace to cram another 5,000 men onto rescue destroyers. The high command pulled out on May 30. A flying boat whisked Freyberg away, and the others went by ship, but not everyone escaped. About 5,500 troops remained on the beach on May 31, when the British naval commander on the scene decided to break off the evacuation. He expected the Luftwaffe to appear at any moment and regarded the risk to his ships as unacceptable. Around nine o'clock in the morning on June 1, the first Germans came down the cliffs and accepted the surrender of the mass of defeated men.

For Britain and its allies, Crete was yet another stunning defeat. Hitler had secured his southern flank and gained a valuable staging ground from which his legions could wreak havoc in the eastern Mediterranean. Around 16,000 of the island's defenders had been lost, including almost 12,000 captured. For the first time in years, an enemy had driven the Royal Navy from one of its private preserves. Three cruisers and six destroyers had been sunk, another seven warships had been heavily damaged, and nearly 2,000 sailors had died. The British naval presence in the Mediterranean had been reduced to a skeleton, and little hope glimmered of immediate re-

Hurrying to aid the supposedly desperate paratroopers at Heraklion, mountain troops remove a stone barricade from the coast road. When the relief column reached the city on May 30, it found the paratroopers in control; the Allied garrison had pulled out two nights earlier.

German paratroopers bury their dead shoulder to shoulder in a mass grave. "I remember Crete as the place of black corpses," one veteran said. "The stink of decay was everywhere."

inforcement. The world wondered how long Great Britain could absorb such staggering losses, in morale as well as in personnel and matériel.

Yet Crete was a Pyrrhic victory for the Third Reich. The Luftwaffe had lost almost 100 combat planes, and—far more devastating—210 transports had been destroyed or severely damaged. They would be sorely missed in Russia. The ground forces had lost more than 4,000 dead, most of them on the first day. Before the battle ended, nearly half of the proud 7th Paratroop Division had been killed or wounded; the Sturmregiment alone left 830 men and 45 officers dead on the field. Some of Germany's most promising young combat leaders were gone. The price of Crete was so high that a number of senior officers considered it the Wehrmacht's first defeat.

Instead of vaulting Kurt Student's elite corps to greater prominence, the invasion had eroded Hitler's confidence in the parachute tactic. The Führer was reported "most displeased with the whole affair." In mid-July, Student and Ringel flew to Hitler's headquarters in East Prussia to receive decorations for valor on Crete. After the ceremony, Hitler bluntly told Student: "Crete has proved that the days of the paratrooper are over. The parachute weapon depends on surprise. The surprise factor has now gone."

Student persisted. He soon proposed an airborne assault on Cyprus as a prelude to an airborne attack on the Suez Canal, but Hitler rejected the idea because of the losses on Crete. The Führer later toyed with the idea of a massive air and sea invasion of the strategic Mediterranean island of Malta. In July of 1942, Student flew to Berlin for a final conference and came away bitterly disappointed. "When I went in to see the Führer," Student reported, "he simply turned it down flat. 'The affair will go wrong and cost too many lives,' he said."

Never again would the blossoming parachutes of the 7th Paratroop Division fill the sky over enemy territory. Except for a few isolated actions and the hit-and-run commando raids that Student abhorred, the paratroopers would fight the rest of the war as ordinary infantry.

Nor had the island invasion brought any lasting strategic gains for Germany, apart from enhancing the security of the Rumanian oil fields. Hitler never pursued the opportunity to dominate the eastern Mediterranean, and Crete became little more than a graveyard. Julius Ringel offered an epitaph: "This sacrifice," he said, "would not have been too great if the Crete campaign had meant a beginning, not an end." ✚

Members of the Wehrmacht who participated in the battle for Crete received this sleeve band, decorated with Mediterranean acanthus leaves in yellow thread on a white cloth background. Survivors of the campaign wore the band on the left cuff of their uniform jackets and overcoats.

From his improvised headquarters on the flank of Regiment Hill, Colonel Bruno Bräuer *(third from left)* watches the Luftwaffe

bomb British positions at Heraklion.

Stranded at Heraklion

When Colonel Bruno Bräuer parachuted into the landing zone assigned to his 1st Paratroop Regiment, east of the Cretan city of Heraklion, he discovered that there, as elsewhere on Crete on May 20, the carefully planned German airborne assault had gone awry.

The medieval walled town was the largest on the island, and the nearby airfield represented one of the most important objectives of General Kurt Student's invasion force. Bräuer hoped to quickly overwhelm Heraklion's garrison by launching simultaneous airborne attacks with three battalions of his own unit, plus a battalion from the 2d Paratroop Regiment. But delays and poor communications combined with an unexpectedly fierce resistance to turn the attack into a bloody shambles. Scores of soldiers were hit before they reached the ground, and those who landed alive were caught in a deadly cross fire of artillery and machine guns. Bräuer's 2d Battalion was nearly annihilated, and a platoon from Major Erich Walther's 1st Battalion, which reached the heights east of the airfield, was also wiped out. The 3d Battalion managed to fight its way into Heraklion, but counterattacking British and Greek troops quickly drove it out. Enraged Cretan peasants wielding antiquated muskets and butcher knives massacred at least one German platoon.

By the end of the third day of fighting, more than half of Bräuer's 2,000 men had been killed, and many others wounded or captured. Scattered over the boulder-strewn hills in isolated detachments, the paratroopers found themselves besieged by an enemy that outnumbered them eight to one. Hidden by darkness, Bräuer was able to consolidate the remnants of his force on high ground a mile and a half south of the airfield. There, the Germans dug in, determined to prevail.

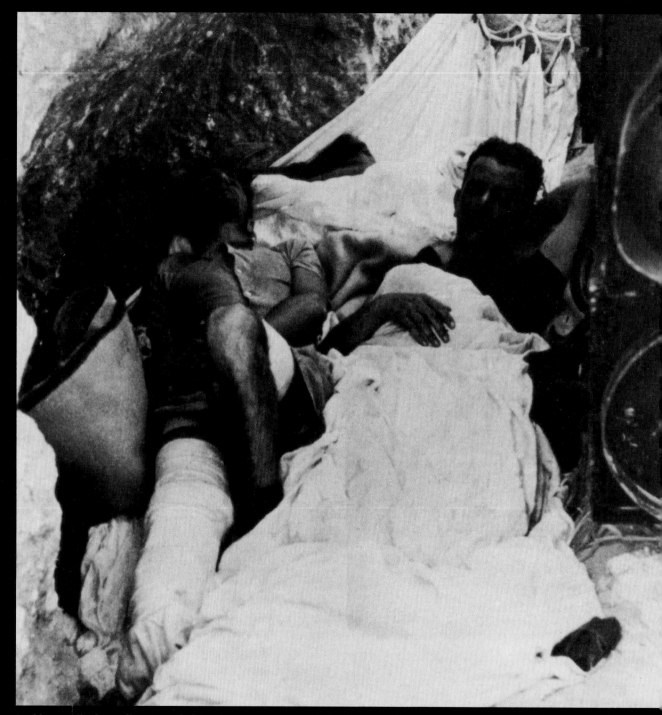

Lacking medical supplies, wounded German paratroopers sheltering in a hillside cave use parachutes as blankets and bandage

Enduring the Strain of Isolation

The week-long battle for Heraklion pushed the German paratroopers to the limits of physical and mental endurance. A lack of food and po-table water compounded their suf-ferings. Rations were reduced to one piece of bread and two ciga-rettes a day, and contaminated wa-ter caused diarrhea throughout the command. By day, the slightest movement drew enemy fire, and isolated foragers risked death at the hands of Cretan partisans.

The strain began to tax the sol-diers. "The faces of some of them grew taut, almost shrunken," one paratrooper recalled. "Their eyes lay deep in their sockets, and their beards, unshaven now for five days, accentuated the hollowness of their cheeks." Only night brought relief. It was then that the wounded were recovered, the dead buried, and the meager rations issued.

Coatless in the heat, Colonel Bräuer radios orders to his embattled battalions. When batteries failed, runners were sent out.

Seeking shade under a parachute shelter, Colonel Bräuer and his officers assess their situation at Heraklion.

A Slender Aerial Lifeline

Colonel Bruno Bräuer's paratroopers at Heraklion were sustained—but barely—by a desperate Luftwaffe supply effort. In order to reach the isolated German troops, the cargo planes had to fly dangerously low. Even so, many of the loads missed the target, and the frustrated men could only watch as the twin-chuted supply canisters drifted down behind enemy lines. Many a British and Greek defender equipped himself with arms and ammunition that were intended for Bräuer's soldiers.

Yet in the end, the sheer persistence of the German fliers paid dividends. Transports dropped several hundred reinforcements, along with mortars that enabled Bräuer's troops to shell British positions. One dauntless pilot even crash-landed his Ju 52 on a hilltop to deliver a field gun and its crew.

Paratroopers steer a donkey laden with ammunition to the battle lines east of Heraklion.

Skimming the parched ground, a Ju 52 drops supply canisters near German positions on Regiment Hill.

Bathed in the broiling sun, shirtless German machine gunners watch the bombardment of the "Two Charlies," a strategic ridge east of Heraklion that was held by a battalion of Australians.

Colonel Bräuer (*in peaked cap*), confers with his wounded and exhausted men under a bridge abutment. "Not one among us would think of doubting our final victory," a German said. "We are tougher than the British."

"No One Doubts Our Final Victory"

Unable to overwhelm the numerically superior Allied force but emboldened by their foe's inertia, Bräuer's paratroopers harassed the enemy with relentless machine-gun and mortar fire. On May 25, the Germans observed with satisfaction as Stukas pounded Heraklion into dusty rubble. The following day, advancing elements of the 2d Paratroop Regiment secured a key hill overlooking the enemy airfield.

The resolve of the German troops stiffened. When the British demanded surrender, one of Bräuer's battalion commanders, Major Karl-Lothar Schulz, responded with a curt note. "The German army has been ordered to occupy Crete," he wrote. "It will obey this order."

Capture of an Abandoned City

Encouraged by the promise of reinforcement, Colonel Bräuer issued orders on the night of May 28 for a full-scale assault at dawn. When the Germans moved, they found Heraklion and its airfield abandoned; the Royal Navy had evacuated the Allies under cover of darkness.

Later that day, troops of the 5th Mountain Division, dispatched to relieve Bräuer's beleaguered command, arrived to discover the paratroopers in full possession of their objective. "It is a strange feeling," one survivor noted, "to be able to walk erect again without bullets whistling by all the time."

Major Karl-Lothar Schulz, commander of the 3d Battalion, 1st Paratroop Regiment, confronts the mayor of Heraklion following the city's occupation.

Major Erich Walther (*left*), Colonel Bruno Bräuer (*top right*), and colleagues rest after the ordeal.

After the Allies evacuated, German paratroopers make their way down a street in Heraklion on a captured British truck.

Acknowledgments

The editors thank: England: London—Alan Williams, Mike Willis, The Imperial War Museum. Federal Republic of Germany: Alsfeld—Walter Gericke. Berlin—Heidi Klein, Bildarchiv Preussischer Kulturbesitz; Gabrielle Kohler, Jürgen Raible, Archiv für Kunst und Geschichte; Wolfgang Streubel, Ullstein Bilderdienst. Dillishausen—

Alex Buchner. Freiburg—Florian Berberich, Militärgeschichtliches Forschungsamt. Koblenz—Meinrad Nilges, Bundesarchiv. Munich—Elisabeth Heidt, Süddeutscher Verlag Bilderdienst. Osnabrück—Helmut Thöle, Munin Verlag. Rösrath-Hoffnungsthal —Helga Müller. Schongau—Rudolf Donth. German Democratic Republic: Berlin—

Hannes Quaschinsky, ADN-Zentralbild. Italy: Milan—Alfredo Hummel. United States: District of Columbia—Elizabeth Hill, National Archives; Eveline Nave, Library of Congress. Yugoslavia: Belgrade—Dragan Kuprešanin, Museum of Revolution; Pavle Ljumović, Army Museum. Zagreb—Ruda Polšak, Museum of Revolution of Croatia.

Picture Credits

Bibliography

Books

Angolia, John R., *For Führer and Fatherland: Military Awards of the Third Reich*. San Jose, Calif.: R. James Bender, 1976.

Ansel, Walter, *Hitler and the Middle Sea*. Durham: Duke University Press, 1972.

Bailey, Ronald H., and the Editors of Time-Life Books, *Partisans and Guerrillas* (World War II series). Alexandria, Va.: Time-Life Books, 1978.

Bekker, Cajus, *The Luftwaffe War Diaries*. Transl. and ed. by Frank Ziegler. Garden City, N.Y.: Doubleday, 1968.

Berberich, Florian, *Unternehmen "Merkur" (Operation "Scorcher"): Die Schlacht um Kreta, 20. Mai bis 1. Juni 1941*. Vol. 5 of *Operationen des Zweiten Weltkrieges*. Forthcoming.

Böhmler, Rudolf, and Werner Haupt, *Fallschirmjäger (Paratrooper)*. Dorheim, W.Ger.: Verlag Hans-Henning Podzun, 1971.

Buchner, Alex:
Die Deutsche Gebirgstruppe, 1939-1945. Dorheim, W.Ger.: Podzun-Verlag, 1971.
Der Deutsche Griechenland-Feldzug. Heidelberg: Kurt Vowinckel Verlag, 1957.
Gebirgsjäger an Allen Fronten. Hanover: Adolf Sponholtz Verlag, 1954.

Clark, Alan, *The Fall of Crete*. New York: William Morrow, 1962.

Cruickshank, Charles, *Greece, 1940-1941*. Newark, Del.: University of Delaware Press, 1976.

Davin, D. M., *Crete*. Wellington, New Zealand: War History Branch, Department of Internal Affairs, 1953.

Edwards, Roger, *German Airborne Troops, 1936-45*. London: Macdonald and Jane's, 1974.

Farrar-Hockley, Anthony, *Student*. New York: Ballantine Books, 1973.

Generalkommando XVIII. (Gebirgs-) A. K. und Stellv. Generalkommando XVIII. A. K., *Gebirgsjäger in Griechenland und auf Kreta*. Berlin: Verlag "Die Wehrmacht," n.d.

The German Campaigns in the Balkans, Spring 1941. Washington, D.C.: Center of Military History, United States Army, 1986.

Green, William, *The Warplanes of the Third Reich*. Garden City, N.Y.: Doubleday, 1972.

Heiss, Friedrich, *Der Sieg im Südosten*. Berlin: Volk und Reich Verlag, 1943.

Hitchens, Marilynn Giroux, *Germany, Russia, and the Balkans: Prelude to the Nazi-Soviet Non-Aggression Pact*. Boulder, Colo.: East European Monographs, 1983.

Kiriakopoulos, G. C., *Ten Days to Destiny*. New York: Franklin Watts, 1985.

Knox, MacGregor, *Mussolini Unleashed, 1939-1941*. Cambridge: Cambridge University Press, 1982.

Kuhn, Volkmar, *German Paratroops in World War II*. Shepperton, England: Ian Allan, 1978.

Kurowski, Franz, *Der Kampf um Kreta*. Herford, W.Ger.: Maximilian-Verlag, 1965.

Lehmann, Rudolf, *The Leibstandarte*. Transl. by Nick Olcott. Winnipeg, Canada: J. J. Fedorowicz, 1987.

Littlejohn, David, and C. M. Dodkins, *Orders, Decorations, Medals and Badges of the Third Reich*. Mountain View, Calif.: R. James Bender, 1970.

Lucas, James, *Alpine Elite*. London: Jane's, 1980.

Makrygiannes, Nikos, *Crete, 1941: The Twilight of Hope* (in Greek). N.p., n.d.

Mellenthin, F. W. von, *Panzer Battles*. Transl. by H. Betzler, ed. by L. C. F. Turner. Norman: University of Oklahoma Press, 1964.

Mitchell, Ruth, *The Serbs Choose War*. Garden City, N.Y.: Doubleday, 1943.

Müller, Günther, and Fritz Scheuering, *Sprung über Kreta*. Oldenburg, W.Ger.: Gerhard Stalling Verlag, 1944.

Murray, Williamson, *Strategy for Defeat: The Luftwaffe, 1933-1945*. Secaucus, N.J.: Chartwell, 1986.

Pack, S. W. C., *The Battle for Crete*. Annapolis, Md.: Naval Institute Press, 1973.

Piekalkiewicz, Janusz, *Krieg auf dem Balkan, 1940-1945*. Munich: Südwest Verlag, 1984.

Rich, Norman, *Hitler's War Aims*. New York: W. W. Norton, 1973.

Roon, Arnold von, *Die Bildchronik der Fallschirmtruppe, 1935-1945*. Friedberg, W.Ger.: Podzun-Pallas-Verlag, 1985.

Shores, Christopher, and Brian Cull, *Air War for Yugoslavia, Greece and Crete*. London: Grub Street, 1987.

Spencer, John Hall, *Battle for Crete*. London: White Lion, 1976.

Stewart, I. McD. G., *The Struggle for Crete, 20 May-1 June 1941*. London: Oxford University Press, 1966.

Student, Kurt, ed., *Kreta: Sieg der Kühnsten*. Graz: Steirische Verlagsanstalt, 1942.

Thomas, David A., *Crete, 1941: The Battle at Sea*. London: André Deutsch, 1972.

Whiting, Charles, *Hunters from the Sky: The German Parachute Corps, 1940-1945*. New York: Stein and Day, 1974.

Other Publications

National Archives. German Military Documents Section:
Einsatz Kreta (Operation Crete). XI Air Corps Battle Report, 11 June 1941.
War diaries and reports of the 5th and 6th Mountain Divisions, together with reports of 85, 100, and 141 Mountain Regiments.

Oberkommando der Wehrmacht, "Völkerrechtsverletzungen der Feindmächte beim Deutschen Einsatz auf Kreta." German Military Archives, Koblenz.

Pallud, Jean Paul, "Operation Merkur: The German Invasion of Crete." *After the Battle*, no. 47.

U.S. Army Military History Institute:
Dinort, Oscar, and Hubertus Hitschhold, "The 2d Stuka Wing in the Crete Operation." MS B-640.
Ringel, Julius, "Capture of Crete, May 1941." MS B-646.
Seibt, Conrad, "The Crete Operation." MS B-641.

Index

Time-Life Books Inc. offers a wide range of fine recordings, including a *Rock 'n' Roll Era* series. For subscription information, call 1-800-621-7026 or write Time-Life Music, P.O. Box C-32068, Richmond, Virginia 23261-2068.